Mormons

Mormons

How to Witness to Them

John R. Farkas
and David A. Reed

Baker Books

A Division of Baker Book House Co
Grand Rapids, Michigan 49516

Published by Baker Books
a division of Baker Book House Company
P.O. Box 6287, Grand Rapids, MI 49516-6287

Printed in the United States of America

Library of Congress Cataloging-in-Publication Data
Farkas, John R.
Mormons : how to witness to them / John R. Farkas and David A. Reed.
   p.   cm.
Includes bibliographical references and indexes.
ISBN 0-8010-5739-6 (pbk.)
   1. Church of Jesus Christ of Latter-Day Saints—Controversial literature. 2. Missions to Mormons. 3. Mormon Church—Controversial literature. I. Reed, David A. II. Title.
BX8645.F38   1997
248.2'4—dc21   97-1616

Some of the materials in chapter 2 and all of appendixes 1–6 were used in *Mormonism: Changes, Contradictions, and Errors* (1995). They are repeated for the convenience of the reader.

For information about academic books, resources for Christian leaders, and all new releases available from Baker Book House, visit our web site:
http://www.bakerbooks.com

Contents

Preface

The Mormon Church, the Church of Jesus Christ of Latter-day Saints, is one of the fastest growing churches in the United States and the world. Nearly 49,000 (at the end of 1995) full-time missionaries help produce this growth. From 1981 through the end of 1991 the Church grew 64 percent worldwide, while in the United States it grew 42 percent.[1] Its worldwide membership was reported at nearly 9.3 million by the end of 1995[2] with about 4.6 million of these in the United States. Through its extensive public relations programs, the Church has gained a general public acceptance unparalleled in its history.

This public acceptance has probably been aided by increasing spiritual ignorance among Christians in our country. Churches across the United States are reporting lower attendance at Sunday schools and Sunday evening services. At the same time, public schools have been teaching reliance on feelings when evaluating events in our lives. Concurrently there has been a trend among mainline Christian pastors toward accepting "liberal Christian" thinking—lifestyles and teachings that would have been rejected twenty-five years ago. This reliance on feelings, along with ignorance or rejection of Christian teachings, works to the advantage of Mormon missionaries. Their teaching approach puts an emphasis on the use of feelings in evaluating their message.[3]

A sound examination and study of Mormonism should put aside feelings and public opinion and instead be factual, historical, and biblical. This book, as did our previous books, will take this approach. Years ago, the top leadership of the Mormon Church did not hesitate to challenge people to examine the teachings of their Church. Debates between top Mormon leaders and non-Mormons were not unusual. Today they are. Below are three examples of challenges by top Mormon leaders. Note that they invite outsiders to "**convince us of our errors,**" "**compare** the religion of the Latter-day Saints," and "if Joseph Smith was a deceiver . . . then **he should be exposed.**" Particularly note "there would appear **many errors and contradictions.**" This book accepts this challenge by exposing such errors and contradictions. Past Mormon leaders said the following:

> . . . **convince us of our errors of doctrine,*** if we have any, by reason, by logical arguments, or by the word of God. . . . (Apostle Orson Pratt, *The Seer* [Jan. 1853], 15)

> I say to the whole world, **receive the truth, no matter who presents it** to you. Take up the Bible, compare the religion of the Latter-day Saints with it, and **see if it will stand the test.** (President Brigham Young, *Journal of Discourses* [May 1873] 16:46)

> **If Joseph Smith was a deceiver, . . . then he should be exposed;** his claims should be refuted, and his doctrines shown to be false, . . . If his claims and declarations were built upon fraud and deceit, **there would appear many errors and contradictions,** which would be easy to detect. The doctrines of false teachers will not stand the test when tried by the accepted standards of measurement, the scriptures. (Apostle Joseph Fielding Smith, *Doctrines of Salvation* [1954], 1:188)

This book has been prepared to help you respond to this challenge. Chapter 1, "Witnessing to Mormons," provides the Bible verses that support witnessing and discusses guidelines and sev-

---

*Bold type and underlined text in quotes are added for emphasis. Items in brackets [ ] are given for additional information.

eral approaches. Other essential parts of the necessary full foundation that must be developed for an effective witness are found in chapter 2, "Introduction to Mormonism." This section outlines the doctrine, history, and authority structure of the Church of Jesus Christ of Latter-day Saints and includes a brief review of its authoritative publications. This is followed by claims and statements by top Mormon Church leaders about the importance of following them.

Chapter 3 discusses the best subjects for witnessing to new Mormons and potential converts. The foundation is completed in chapters 4 through 6 with subjects that can be effective in reaching seasoned Mormons, help in answering their questions, and questions to ask Mormons.

Acknowledgments

We thank Phyllis Farkas for her continued dedication, comments, and corrections to the manuscript.

We have a great appreciation for and gratitude to the writers and researchers who have walked this same path before us for making their information available.

Above all, we are ever grateful for the help we have received from the Holy Spirit and for our opportunity to witness for the truth of the gospel of our Lord and Savior Jesus Christ.

1

Witnessing to Mormons

Certain biblical and practical considerations provide basic guidelines for witnessing. The general principles laid out below should be considered and applied, as appropriate, when witnessing to a Mormon or someone interested in Mormonism. Later chapters will present suitable subject matter for such discussions, but the guidelines presented here need to be followed so that your discussions proceed smoothly and accomplish their goal.

A prerequisite to any witnessing, not just witnessing to Mormons, is to know and understand what God's Word, the Bible, says on the subject. Without this foundation, you may be persuaded that you should only say good things about others and that you should only make positive statements about other churches. The Bible is very emphatic on this subject and includes the following admonitions.

What the Bible Says about Witnessing

Warn the wicked

When I say unto the wicked, Thou shalt surely die; and thou givest him not warning, nor speakest to warn the wicked from his wicked

13

way, to save his life; the same wicked man shall die in his iniquity; but his blood will **I require at thine hand.** Yet **if thou warn** the wicked, and he turn not from his wickedness, nor from his wicked way, he shall die in his iniquity; but thou hast delivered thy soul. (Ezek. 3:18–19)

Teach all nations

Go ye therefore, and **teach all nations,** baptizing them in the name of the Father, and of the Son, and of the Holy Ghost. (Matt. 28:19)

Be ready to give an answer in meekness

But sanctify the Lord God in your hearts: and **be ready always to give an answer** to every man that asketh you a reason of the hope that is in you **with meekness and fear.** (1 Peter 3:15)

Preach, reprove, rebuke, exhort, with longsuffering and doctrine

Preach the word; be instant in season, out of season; reprove, rebuke, exhort with all longsuffering and doctrine. (2 Tim. 4:2)

Discern good and evil

But strong meat belongeth to them that are of full age, even those who by reason of use have their senses exercised **to discern both good and evil.** (Heb. 5:14)

Contend for the faith

Beloved, when I gave all diligence to write unto you of the common salvation, it was needful for me to write unto you, and exhort you that ye should **earnestly contend for the faith** which was once delivered unto the saints. (Jude 3)

Reason and dispute daily in the market and synagogue

Now when they had passed through Amphipolis and Apollonia, they came to Thessalonica, where was a synagogue of the Jews: And Paul, as his manner was, **went in** unto them, and three sabbath days **reasoned with them** out of the scriptures, . . . Therefore **disputed** he in the synagogue with the Jews, and with the devout persons, and **in the market daily** with them that met with him. (Acts 17:1–2, 17)

And he **reasoned** in the synagogue every sabbath, and **persuaded** the Jews and the Greeks. (Acts 18:4)

And he went into the synagogue, and **spake boldly** for the space of three months, **disputing and persuading** the things concerning the kingdom of God. But when divers were hardened, and believed not, but spake evil of that way before the multitude, he departed from them, and separated the disciples, **disputing daily in the school of one Tyrannus.** (Acts 19:8–9)

Be gentle, patient, meek while instructing

And the servant of the Lord must not strive; but **be gentle unto all men,** apt to teach, **patient,** In **meekness instructing** those that oppose themselves; if God peradventure will give them repentance to the acknowledging of the truth; And that they may recover themselves out of the snare of the devil, who are taken captive by him at his will. (2 Tim. 2:24–26)

In addition to these directions from the Bible, we recommend that your witness be born of God: "Not by might, nor by power, but by my spirit, saith the LORD of hosts" (Zech. 4:6). This can happen only if you pray asking the Lord for his direction, seeking what he wants you to do. "For we are his workmanship, created in Christ Jesus unto good works, which God hath before ordained **that we should walk in them**" (Eph. 2:10). Face-to-face witnessing to the lost is a calling from the Lord. It may be that your calling is not in this area but in supporting those doing it. Whatever your calling, you should let the Lord guide you to it.

If you are called to witnessing, it should be based on clear factual knowledge about Mormonism, not hearsay or feelings. One of the main purposes of this book is to arm you with this accurate information.

Your witnessing should be based on a solid Christian foundation, the Bible. It is important to know your own beliefs and to be confident in them. If you do not know exactly what you believe, why you believe it, and where to find it in the Bible, you should not alone undertake witnessing to a mature Mormon. *Seek experienced help.*

Your witnessing should be based on a deep concern and Christian love for the person you want to help. Remember, the person you are witnessing to is not your enemy. If your purpose is to win arguments or to put people down, then you are not doing it for the Lord and you should not be witnessing.

Expectations

When you are witnessing, you have responsibilities to the person you are witnessing to; and in a similar way, whether they acknowledge it or not, they have responsibilities to you. The Golden Rule is a good approach at all times. You should reasonably expect the following, at least from yourself.

Never be rude and never use ridicule. Always be polite. The following verses should guide you: "A soft answer turneth away wrath: but grievous words stir up anger" (Prov. 15:1); and "A brother offended is harder to be won than a strong city: and their contentions are like the bars of a castle" (Prov. 18:19).

Don't let yourself get drawn into an angry argument. Walk away from an irrational or heated discussion.

Be ready to provide references, and even copies of key pages of Mormon works to support information you present about what Mormon leaders have said or done.[1] It is reasonable to expect the same from the person you are dealing with. *Look up biblical references they give you* (and other references if possible) to verify their actual wording and their context and, hence, their true meaning. Out-of-context quotes often do not mean what we are led to believe.

Don't try to cover too many subjects at one meeting. It is better to cover a few subjects well (reaching definite conclusions if possible) than to skim over a multitude of subjects without fully addressing the issues. Making this happen will require your close attention. It is very easy to get pulled into another subject prematurely. Keep a paper nearby and say something like, "Since we are now talking about (name the subject), I'll write down this new subject and we'll cover it later if you wish." Or you might say, "I'm not prepared to talk about (name the subject), so let's put it off until (set a time)."

Be sure the person is interested. After your discussion is underway, you may realize that the person you are speaking with is only interested in arguing or taking up your time. When this is evident ask: "If you are wrong, would you like to know it?" If the answer is a clear no, even after you test for understanding, then stop the discussion. There is no point in continuing.

Other Witnessing Considerations

The following principles should also play a key role when witnessing.

Pray privately and then, if possible, pray with the Mormon(s) you will be witnessing to, both before and after a discussion. You or another Christian should say the prayer and use it as an opportunity to teach Christian principles.

Be prepared. Do your homework. Know your Bible and the subject(s) you plan to cover. You do not have to learn the Mormon subjects all at once. You only need to be a few hours or so ahead of the person you will be witnessing to. If you get onto a subject you don't know or are not sure of, say so, and then do your homework for the next meeting.

Use only the King James Version of the Bible. This is the official version used by the Mormon Church and by using it you eliminate one source of contention.

Know the meaning of LDS terminology (see appendix 2) and avoid using Christian jargon because you may be saying one thing and the Mormon may be understanding another. For example:

Do not ask: "If you were to die now would you go to heaven?"
Instead ask: "If you were to die now, would you spend eternity with God?" (Mormons conceive of heaven as multi-tiered, with God inhabiting the highest level.)

Do not ask: "Are you saved?"
Instead ask: "Is Jesus Christ your Lord and Savior and through your faith in him and his grace will you spend eternity with

him?" (The Mormon concept of salvation is complex and entirely different from what Christians mean when they say they are saved.)

Know what the Mormon Scriptures, called the standard works, *are.* Not all new and old Mormon references and authors are of equal authority, and some should not be used at all. These are covered in chapter 2 under "Authoritative Publications."

Do not assume that the Mormons you deal with know Mormon doctrine. Expect a broad spectrum of beliefs. Many have very little knowledge and understanding of the unique teachings of their church. Others will know them all and say so. Still others may know the differences but try to hide them and appear knowledgeable. Be prepared for cases where you are divulging information about the LDS Church never before heard or understood by the Mormon. You should not say: "You believe . . ." (unless you know the person's beliefs from earlier in the conversation). It is best to say: "The Mormon Church teaches . . . Do you believe this?" The Mormon may not believe the Church actually has taught certain things without seeing it in print—in either original LDS publications or photocopies from them.

Do not accept general statements like "The Bible is all wrong" or "You people only deal in half truths and misrepresentations" or similar assertions. Insist on specific references. Consider abandoning discussion with those who consistently refuse to deal in specifics.

Use a slow, low-key, soft, friendly approach. You do not want to intimidate your contact. If you will only have opportunity for one meeting, cover the subjects in a little less detail and with more boldness until you run out of time. You may plant more seeds this way. In some cases you may not have your notes and references nearby and setting up an appointment or exchanging addresses may not appear possible. You will have to rely on your memory and the Holy Spirit. In this case, you should just cover what you can in the time you have. A soft-spoken, loving witness, even in this situation, is better than nothing and may lead to additional discussions.

Discuss only important topics, like the ones we cover in this book. Do not waste time with trivia.

Know that certain things are stumbling blocks to Mormons; for example, tea, coffee, alcohol, tobacco. It is best not to use these while witnessing.

Never agree to the request that you pray about the Book of Mormon. The reasons are covered at the end of chapter 2, under "Evaluating Truth."

One possible technique with Mormon missionaries and others is to *invite them into your home for a meal.* Let them know the eating time, but ask them to come an hour or two early and use this time for discussion. With the meal as an enticement, they are less likely to suddenly have another appointment.[2]

Expect significant resistance, so—as previously pointed out—be ready to use the big question when appropriate: "If you are wrong, would you like to know it?" If the answer is a clear no, even after you test for understanding, then stop witnessing.

Various Approaches to Witnessing

As your knowledge of Mormonism and how to witness increases in depth and breadth, you may note that there are several approaches or topics that can be used. These overlap somewhat, but they can be differentiated as follows.

The historical method. This involves focusing on inconsistencies in the Mormon story—alterations in what the LDS Church has presented as fact. Examples would include the First Vision story, the temple ceremony, teachings about men of African heritage (Blacks), false prophecies by Mormon leaders, and changes to scriptures.

Doctrinal comparisons. This approach deals primarily with significant contradictory changes to Mormon doctrine. It may involve contrasting the God of the Book of Mormon with the God of the other LDS scriptures and the Bible, contrasting the early Mormon Church's concept of God with their present teachings, or comparison of the God of the present Mormon Church to the God of the Bible. The latter is usually more effective with non-Mormons and new Mormons, but it should also be used with mature Mormons.

The Book of Mormon. This approach involves pointing out changes that can be observed by comparing an original 1830 edition of the Book of Mormon to a current edition and highlighting differences between present teachings of the Mormon Church and what is actually found and not found in the Book of Mormon.

People experienced in Mormon studies and witnessing to Mormons may use all of the above approaches, sometimes concentrating their efforts more in one direction than another. Chapters 3 to 5 provide examples of each approach.

Speaking to others about Mormonism requires flexibility—ideally each person should be given a customized approach. But this is not possible until more is learned about the needs of each one. Many times this is not easily accomplished. But it is usually possible early on to divide people into two groups: those who know little about Mormonism and those who are very knowledgeable. In some cases, the length of time people have been in the Mormon Church has little to do with their comprehension of Mormon doctrine. Some active Mormon women who have not had Mormon husbands seem to have a much lower understanding of LDS teachings.

Indirect Witnessing

Many people who do not feel called to direct face-to-face witnessing to Mormons are still able to help in other ways. Some actively support those who can witness. They provide food and housing, give cash donations, donate items that those who are witnessing can use (like books and other literature), arrange for meetings with those who can benefit (Mormons, those getting interested in Mormonism).

Others engage in indirect witnessing by educating Christians and others about the errors of Mormonism, by placing warning papers in Mormon books in public libraries, or by writing letters in response to articles on Mormonism in newspapers and magazines. As in the case of face-to-face encounters, indirect witnessing calls for a loving and tactful approach, with Mormon teachings as the target rather than the Mormon people.

2

Introduction to Mormonism

Before getting into the major problems with Mormonism, it is first necessary to continue to build the foundation of information started in chapter 1. This will be needed to help you understand the Latter-day Saints' (LDS) thinking on certain key subjects, such as what the Mormons may not say to you, the role of feelings in determining truth, and the LDS teachings about the reliability of the Bible.

A basic understanding of the Mormon religion cannot be gained apart from a study of the movement's history, a grasp of the unique vocabulary members use, and an appreciation of the authority structure of the LDS Church.

Mormon History

Although the organizational and doctrinal history of Mormonism is a complicated subject, it is a necessary part of the foundational information that needs to be absorbed if you are to witness effectively. Available publications on the subject fill many bookshelves, and the more you read, the better (see appendix 6 for suggestions). To use the topics for witnessing covered in this book, however, you need only study the detailed chronology of the major events in Mormon history found in appendix 2. It should be carefully studied.

Unique Mormon Terminology

Understanding the unique vocabulary (and related doctrine) used by the Mormon Church in its teaching manuals, scriptures, and talks by its top leaders is another part of the foundation that must support your witnessing. Some of these words and doctrines are unlikely to be mentioned by Mormon missionaries or in LDS publicity. Some terms and expressions are exactly the same as those used by Christians, but are used with different meanings.

Our intent here is not to provide a biblical answer to the Mormon teachings. That has already been done in our book *Mormons Answered Verse by Verse*. Appendix 3 outlines the unique Mormon Church teachings needed to prepare you for the subjects in the following chapters. These should also be studied carefully.

Authority in the Mormon Church

Within the Mormon Church, authority flows from the top down. The organization is structured in what might be called a classical pyramid shape, with the point upward. The President of the Church (always a man), with his counselors (usually two, always men), together form the First Presidency, the point or tip of the pyramid. The President is also called the Prophet, Seer, and Revelator. He is the only one in the Church who has full authority and "keys," and the *only one* who can speak for God and receive revelation for the Church. According to Bruce R. McConkie in *Mormon Doctrine*:

> He is the earthly head of the kingdom of God, the supreme officer of the Church, the "President of the High Priesthood of the Church. . . ." His duty is to preside over the whole church and to be like unto Moses. . . . (p. 591)[1]

High-level leaders in the Mormon Church under the Prophet are called the General Authorities,[2] and each gets his authority for assigned responsibilities from the President/Prophet.

The Quorum of the Twelve Apostles, twelve men just under the prophet, also have the same authority and "keys" as the president, but can only partially use them as authorized by the president. President Joseph F. Smith, in *Gospel Doctrine,* said, "What is a key?[3] It is the right or privilege which belongs to and comes with the Priesthood, to have communication with God" (p. 422). Such keys can only be fully used by the apostles when there is no president, and that historically has seldom happened for long periods.

The Quorum of the Seventy forms the next level below the apostles. As of October 1, 1994, there were seventy-nine men in this body (in two quorums), but vacancies sometimes go unfilled for a period of time.

Within the Mormon Church only men can hold the priesthood. They are the only ones with the formal authority to act in God's name. (But the role of women can be considered significant in that the priesthood holder cannot reach exaltation unless married to a woman in the temple for time and eternity.) Apostle Bruce R. McConkie said, ". . . priesthood is the power and authority of God delegated to man on earth to act in all things for the salvation of men" (*Mormon Doctrine*, p. 594).

At the local level, a Mormon congregation is called a "ward." Headed by a bishop and his two counselors, the ward is the level at which the Mormon Church carries out most of its programs. A congregation not large or stable enough to support all the usual activities is called a "branch" and is headed by a branch president. Several branches and wards form a "stake." A stake is similar to a diocese in the Catholic Church, and is led by a stake president and his two counselors.

Authoritative Publications

There are many publications a person could read to ascertain the teachings of the Mormon Church. They include the canonized scriptures (King James Version of the Bible, Book of Mormon, Doctrine and Covenants, Pearl of Great Price) as well as official sermons and talks by the President and other top leaders as found in official Church teaching manuals, books, magazines, and newspapers and in privately published newspapers, books, and papers. Most of the books are printed by the Mormon Church's publishing house, Deseret Book Company, or by private companies such as Bookcraft, Incorporated, of Salt Lake City. A wide range of materials is available from a variety of sources. Pamphlets, tracts, audiotapes, and videos are usually directed at nonmembers (for public relations) and therefore do not get into deep Mormon doctrine. It is not possible to rank these publications in rigid order from most authoritative to least authoritative, but the above list does present them in that order in a general way. Elder Boyd K. Packer of the Quorum of the Twelve Apostles, in speaking about the all-important Mormon priesthood, seemed to express the same ideas when he said:

> There are some things about the priesthood that every elder should know if he is to understand how the Church is governed. . . . There are principles and precepts and rules which are often overlooked and seldom taught. Some of these are found in the scriptures, others in the handbooks. Some of them are not found in either. They are found in the Church. You might call them traditions, but they are more than that. They are revelations which came when the brethren of the past assembled themselves, agreed upon his word, and offered their prayers of faith.[4]

The problem of determining the official position of the LDS Church on a given subject is exacerbated by the fact that the Mormon scriptures, the *standard works,* while sometimes described as the only source of doctrine, in many cases do *not* clearly present many of the unique Mormon teachings; in fact, there are instances where they teach just the opposite. For example, the Book of Mormon says nothing about the vicarious work for the dead carried on in Mormon temples (rather it clearly teaches that salvation can be attained in this life only); nothing on eternal progression, the potential of men to progress to become Gods; nothing about God the Father having once been a man capable of physical death (rather it teaches that God is from all eternity to all eternity). Yet all these ideas are presented very clearly in teaching manuals published and copyrighted by the Mormon Church and in talks by top leaders. Teaching manuals are, in fact, the best documents to use in determining official teachings even though they ostensibly rank lower than the Mormon scriptures in authority. Such manuals often spell out doctrines more explicitly than LDS scriptures. Usually they are published by the Mormon Church and copyrighted by the Corporation of the President of the Church of Jesus Christ of Latter-day Saints; therefore, their statements cannot be dismissed as unrepresentative of Mormon doctrine without opening the LDS Church to the criticism of selling useless books.

Further confounding this issue are the assertions by Mormon Church presidents that the president of the Church must be obeyed, *even if wrong.*[5] Doctrine and Covenants 21:4–5 says concerning the prophet leading the Church: "Thou shalt give heed unto **all** his words and commandments which he shall give . . . As if from mine [Jesus Christ's] own mouth. . . ." (author's emphasis).

Because top Mormon leaders spoke with such authority, many collections of their sermons and talks have been published, including teachings by most of the Church presidents. The largest collection can be found in the 26-volume *Journal of Discourses.* Started by the authority of Brigham Young in 1855, this collection covers the years from 1844 to 1886.

Sharing the true gospel of Jesus Christ with a Mormon can be compared to supplying electricity to an electrical appliance. Your extension cord may be plugged into a live outlet, but if the other end does not correspond to the prong configuration on the appliance's plug, you won't be able to make the connection. That's the same problem encountered by Christians who try to witness to Mormons without first learning something about Mormonism: they can't make the connection. The Apostle Paul made the connection for the Greeks in Athens by prefacing the gospel message with references to Greek literature and quotes from earlier Greek religious authorities, all the while using terminology Greeks would understand (see Acts 17:18–31). You can do the same for

Mormons after you become familiar with the basics of their history, their authoritative publications and leaders, and their unique use of words.

Evaluating Truth—by Feelings or the Bible?

Mormon missionaries and members, if given a chance, will ask you to pray about the Book of Mormon. Their favorite references are:

> If any of you lack wisdom, let him ask of God, that giveth to all men liberally, and upbraideth not; and it shall be given him. (James 1:5)

> And when ye shall receive these things, I would exhort you that ye would ask God, the eternal father, in the name of Christ, **if these things are not true; and if ye shall ask with a sincere heart, with real intent, having faith in Christ, he will manifest the truth of it unto you,** by the power of the Holy Ghost. (Moroni 10:4, author's emphasis)

Frequently they quote these with the implication that the person praying need only invest minimal effort in reading and studying the Book of Mormon and rely on prayer to validate the book. But the reader must be very cautious in using these verses. James 1:5 says *if you lack wisdom*, not *if you require knowledge*. In most cases, wisdom is the proper use of knowledge. There is a big difference between *wisdom* and *knowledge*. There are several Greek words for various types of knowledge, and none of these were used in James 1:5. The Greek word for wisdom *(sophia)* was used. In Moroni 10:4 the assumption is that the Book of Mormon is true and you are praying to confirm it; therefore if you obtain a negative answer, you must not have asked *with a sincere heart, with real intent, having faith in Christ*. But this is not the way the Bible tests truth. The Bible warns us about following paths that seem correct, but that lead to fatal error:

There is a way which seemeth right unto a man, but the end thereof are the ways of death. (Prov. 14:12)

In addition, the Bible is very clear that we should use our intellect, our brains, in evaluating religious teachings:[6]

Prove all things; hold fast that which is good. (1 Thess. 5:21)

Beloved, *believe not every spirit,* but *try the spirits* whether they are of God: because many false prophets are gone out into the world. (1 John 4:1)

How do we *prove all things* and *try the spirits?* We compare it to what God has already said in the Bible. We should do what the people in Berea did to evaluate the Apostle Paul's teachings:

And the brethren immediately sent away Paul and Silas by night unto Berea: who coming thither went into the synagogue of the Jews. These were more noble than those in Thessalonica, in that they received the word with all readiness of mind, and *searched the scriptures daily, whether those things were so.* (Acts 17:10–11, author's emphasis)

Study to show thyself approved unto God, a workman that needeth not to be ashamed, rightly dividing the word of truth. (2 Tim. 2:15)

And take the helmet of salvation, and the sword of the spirit, which is the word of God. (Eph. 6:17)

For God hath not given us the spirit of fear; but of power, and of love, and of a sound mind. (2 Tim. 1:7)

Feelings are just one of the ways God confirms his truth for us. But feelings need to be tested against God's Word, keeping in mind that God will never contradict what he has already said.

Are there some things we should not pray about? If you had a sexual urge, would you pray to find out if you should satisfy it with a prostitute? If you quickly needed a large supply of money, would you ask God if you should go rob a bank? If a voice in your head told you to murder someone, would this mean you should? Of course not. The answer is a clear *no!* God has already spoken on these things in his Word (the Holy Bible), so we should not tempt him by asking for a personal answer. It is already clear how we should handle these types of issues. In the same way, we should not automatically pray about the Book of Mormon. We should test the Book of Mormon and the other LDS scriptures against the Bible.

In addition, we recommend that you not try to "invent the wheel" by yourself in your study of the LDS scriptures. The work of research into Mormonism has already been done, and there is a great deal of help available. Appendix 6 has a list of ministries that may help.

3

For Potential Converts and New Mormons

This chapter features material that has proved effective when witnessing to new Mormons and to non-Mormons drawn to the sect, as well as to long-time members who, for one reason or another, are not very knowledgeable about LDS doctrine. The general approach is to show clear and obvious contradictions in Mormon teachings on a variety of subjects, including the nature of God—teachings easily recognized as diametrically opposed to each other and not biblical in some cases. The table at the end of this chapter summarizes most of the references quoted.

The discussion in this chapter about the nature of God is best for witnessing to new Mormons and potential converts due to its ease of understanding. The subject requires little knowledge of Mormonism. The impact is increased if the person you are dealing with also has had some Bible training, but it is not necessary. This is not to say that this discussion cannot be used with knowledgeable Mormons, those who know and accept all the teachings of the LDS Church. This approach can and should be used on this population, but the success rate is better with the first group.

Why the Bible Is Reliable

Among the dangers of Mormonism are the teachings that make adherents hostile to the genuine Christian churches and leave them in confusion about the reliability of the Bible. Details on LDS teachings about the Bible are found in chapter 6 under "Is the Bible Reliable According to the Mormon Church?" Those interested in Mormonism need to be assured that the Bible is reliable.

One of the first things I (John) did after I realized Mormonism was false was to examine the reliability of the Bible by studying books on its history and how we received it. Covering this subject could be a book in itself, so I will just summarize my findings. The following are reasons why I now consider that the Bible is from God and should be used as a rule for faith, salvation, and action.

1. It is logical that God would give us something written.
2. The Bible is inspirational and intrinsically correct and good, and if followed it leads to a quality life.
3. There is good evidence that it was transmitted and handed down to us with only very minor errors, none of which significantly affect meaning. Mormonism's position that significant parts are missing and distorted conflicts with the Bible's own statements, some of which are:

The grass withereth, the flower fadeth: but the word of our God shall stand for ever. (Isa. 40:8)

I will build my church and the gates of hell shall not prevail against it. (Matt. 16:18)

Heaven and earth shall pass away: but my words shall not pass away. (Mark 13:31)

Being born again, not of corruptible seed, but of incorruptible, by the word of God, which liveth and abideth for ever. (1 Peter 1:23)

Neither pray I for these [the apostles] alone, but for them [us] also which shall believe on me through their word. (John 17:20)

And take the helmet of salvation, and the sword of the Spirit, which is the word of God. (Eph. 6:17)

4. Many parts of it are historically and archaeologically verifiable.
5. It is a record of prophecy (Old Testament) and its fulfillment (New Testament).
6. The personal witness and testimony of some of its writers, along with what Jesus' followers did after he died, rose from the grave, and ascended to heaven, speaks clearly of its divine source.

Read the Bible every day (start with the Gospel of John) while considering and studying in depth all the above (and more that you might add). Then pray regularly, asking God to witness the truth of the Bible to you. I prayed to the One True God of all creation, the God of the Old Testament prophets, the God of Abraham, Isaac, Jacob, and Moses. I said I didn't want any counterfeits. Now that you are doing your part, you can expect the Holy Spirit to give you a personal testimony. Remember James 1:5: "If any of you lack wisdom, let him ask of God." And 1 Thessalonians 5:21: "Prove all things; . . ." Note that wisdom is the proper use of knowledge, and we must first do our part in gathering that knowledge before we ask God for the wisdom.

Note that in item 3 above, Mark 13:31 and Matthew 16:18 consist of Jesus' words. If Mormonism is correct in saying that parts are missing from the Bible and are mistranslated and that there was a complete apostasy, then Jesus lied to us. I reject that idea! In 1 Peter 1:23 the Apostle Peter tells us that the Word of God lives and is with us forever! Did he lie? Mormonism seems to say he did. The Mormon Church teaches that shortly after Jesus died, many of his important teachings were lost,[1] but they were restored through Joseph Smith starting in 1830.[2] In John 17:20 we find Jesus in his great intercessory prayer asking the Father to bless those in the future who believe in him through the "word" of the apostles. It is illogical to believe that the Lord's special prayer for the future faithful was honored for a short period and then was ignored for about 1800 years. When the Apostle Paul told us in Ephesians 6:17 to take up "the sword of the Spirit, which is the word of God," was he telling us to take up a defective sword? If Mormonism were correct, we would have to believe this and that our Lord's prayer for us was ignored. We would also have to believe that the Holy Spirit (John 14:26; 16:13; Acts 1:8) was a failure and that the apostles the Lord appointed, and then their disciples and their disciples and so on, were also complete and dismal failures. These ideas are also illogical![3]

What the Mormons Don't Tell Potential Converts

In our interaction with each other, no matter what our beliefs, we need to keep in mind the need for basic honesty. Rochester, New York, Area Realtors encourage the seller of a house to tell the prospective buyer about hidden defects, such as a leaky roof or termites. Some states have a law that requires such a report. There is a federal law that requires that the lender of money make clear up front all the costs the borrower will have to pay. It is called "truth in lending." Shouldn't similar principles apply in transactions that affect a person's soul?

Yet Mormons hand out the Book of Mormon and other Mormon scriptures as if they had no hidden defects, when in fact, several examples come to mind:

1. The Book of Mormon omits many of the very unique teachings of the Mormon Church (these will be detailed below).
2. The present-day Book of Mormon is significantly different from the original 1830 edition. Several doctrinal changes have been made to it. It has been shown that, including punctuation and spelling, almost 4,000 changes have been made to the 1981 edition when compared to the 1830 edition.[4]
3. Doctrine and Covenants contains revelations allegedly given by God on specific dates. Most were given to Joseph Smith between 1820 and 1844. Yet the wording of many of these revelations in today's edition (1981) differs significantly from their wording when first published in the

1833 Book of Commandments and the 1835 Doctrine and Covenants.[5]

Did the LDS missionaries or your Mormon friends tell you about all the unique teachings of the Mormon Church and changes to LDS scripture when they told you about Mormonism? Were they open and honest about these things? Is it really being honest when this type of information is not divulged to a prospective convert? If worldly financial affairs require full disclosure, shouldn't it be so with spiritual things? Certainly affairs that affect the soul deserve as much care and honesty.

We frequently hear from people who have spoken with Mormon missionaries. Many of them have come from such discussions feeling the LDS Church was just another Christian church, with perhaps some minor unique aberrations (baptism for the dead, for example). At the Mormon Church's visitor centers (Hill Cumorah, just south of Palmyra, New York, to name one) a handout titled *The Thirteen Articles of Faith* is presented as if it summarized the teachings of the Mormon Church. Films are shown at the same center projecting a similar idea. By the same token, we have frequently been asked to read the Book of Mormon as if it contained most or all LDS teachings, the fullness of the gospel. We have never been given, or heard of, any official Mormon tract or booklet that openly and briefly summarizes all of their major teachings. In fact, we believe such a document does not exist.[6] Since such teachings can easily be summarized (as we do below) and listed in a booklet, the omission must not be accidental. It must be the LDS Church's policy to conceal its major deviations from traditional Christianity when recruiting new members.

What are these teachings? Examples include these Mormon Church teachings that are *not found* in the Book of Mormon:

1. God the Father has a body of flesh and bones. (In truth, the Book of Mormon teaches that God is a spirit—Mosiah 15:1–5; Alma 18:26–29; 19:25–27; 22:8–11; 31:15–38.)[7]
2. The Father, Son, and Holy Ghost are separate and distinct Gods.

3. They are one God in that they are "one in purpose."
4. God the Father was once a man like us and progressed until he became God. (In reality, the Book of Mormon says God has always been God from eternity to eternity— Mosiah 3:5; 2 Nephi 27:23; 29:9; Moroni 7:22; 8:18; Mormon 9:9, 19.)
5. There are three levels in heaven.
6. We can progress and become Gods with "all the power, glory, dominion, and knowledge" the Father and Son have.
7. The eleborate priesthoods and organization in present-day Mormonism. There is no mention by name of the Aaronic and Melchizedek Priesthood, there are no deacons mentioned at all, there are no ordinations to any priesthood, and in Moroni 6:1 those who appear to hold a priesthood office (by the present criteria) are baptized *after* they show works worthy of it.
8. Our spirits and the spirit of Jesus Christ were born in the pre-existence (a pre-mortal life).
9. The "new and everlasting covenant," temple marriage and the practice of polygamy, are taught in D&C 132. (In fact, the practice of polygamy is condemned by the present-day Mormon Church and by the Book of Mormon: Jacob 2:24, 27; Mosiah 11:2; Ether 10:5.)
10. Matter is eternal, and all Jesus Christ did in his creation was to organize and form it.
11. Vicarious work for the dead is now done in Mormon temples. (In reality, the Book of Mormon rules out such a practice—2 Nephi 26:11; Alma 5:28; 34:31–35; Mosiah 16:5, 11; 26:25–27.)
12. God is married—there is a Mother in heaven.
13. The sacred temple endowment ceremonies that Mormonism teaches are needed to pass through the veil to spend eternity with God.
14. Jesus Christ atoned for our sins in the Garden of Gethsemane. In fact, the Book of Mormon does not even mention the Garden of Gethsemane; it says Jesus Christ died

for all men on the cross—2 Nephi 9:5; 1 Nephi 11:33; 3 Nephi 27:14.

Many of the above teachings are needed, according to an official Mormon Church publication (*Gospel Principles*, pre-1986 editions, pp. 291–293), to allow a person who accepts and lives them to reach exaltation (becoming a God) in the celestial kingdom of God. Is it unreasonable to expect these ideas to be clearly taught prior to baptism?

A review of the six LDS missionary discussions published by the Mormon Church reveals a similar problem.[8] Except for items 1, 5, and 11 above, they also do not clearly teach the items in the above list. Discussion #4 is titled "Eternal Progression," but it gives only an incomplete, sketchy description. Could it be that the gospel of the Mormon Church excludes, or does not contain, the items not taught? No, this is not the case. Mormon Apostle Bruce R. McConkie said:

> The *gospel* of Jesus Christ is the plan of salvation. It embraces **all** of the laws, principles, doctrines, rites, ordinances, acts, powers, authorities, and keys necessary to save and exalt men in the highest heaven hereafter. . . . In the broadest sense, all truth is part of the gospel; for all truth is known to, is ordained by, and comes from Deity. . . . (*Mormon Doctrine*, pp. 331–332)

There are many countries in the world where the Mormon missionaries are present on a full-time basis, and two of the LDS scriptures (Doctrine and Covenants and Pearl of Great Price) are not available in the language of those countries.[9] Perhaps this is intentional, in harmony with the direction given by Joseph Smith in June 1837:

> My instructions to the brethren were, when they arrived in England, to adhere closely to the **first principles of the gospel**, and **remain silent** concerning the gathering, the vision, and the book of doctrine and covenants,[10] until such time as the work was fully established, and it should be clearly made manifest by the spirit to do otherwise. (*History of the Church*, 2:492)

What are the "first principles of the gospel" mentioned by Joseph Smith? In 1842, in *The Articles of Faith*, he said:

> We believe that **the first principles and ordinances of the gospel** are: first, faith in the Lord Jesus Christ; second, Repentance; third, Baptism by immersion for the remission of sins; fourth, Laying on of hands for the gift of the Holy Ghost. (Pearl of Great Price, *Articles of Faith*, #4, p. 60)

But on April 6, 1844, at General Conference he said:

> It is *the first principle of the gospel* to know for a certainty the character of God and to know that we may converse with him as one man converses with another, and that he was once a man like us; yea, that God himself the Father of us all, dwelt on an earth the same as Jesus Christ himself did.... (*History of the Church*, 6:305)

Shouldn't the LDS missionaries be teaching *all* of the "first principles"? Why would Joseph Smith instruct the missionaries to remain silent about certain events and teachings? We are judged not only by what we say and do, but also by what we don't say or do. One has to wonder why the *full* LDS gospel is not proudly and loudly proclaimed everywhere in every country where the Mormons preach. Why do they hold back from making clear public statements on *all* their teachings? Some would say they first have to teach the "milk" of the Mormon gospel and then the "meat" would follow at a later date. If this is the case though, why do they baptize a person into the Mormon Church before all the meat is clearly presented—meat that includes the unique doctrine separating Mormons from traditional Christianity?[11] Is it fair and honest to omit this information? Mormon writer Robert J. Matthews, in a different context, said:

> Even sharing the truth can have the effect of lying when we tell only half-truths that do not give a full picture. We can also be guilty of bearing false witness and lying if we say nothing, particularly if we allow another to reach a wrong conclusion while we hold back information that would have led to a more accurate perception. In this case it is as though an actual lie were uttered.[12]

Why is the Mormon Church's leadership afraid to publicly and openly teach *all* Mormon doctrine prior to baptism? Are they fearful some of it would be labeled non-Christian and people would not join? We think this is the case.

Archaeology and the Book of Mormon

Places, People, Cities, and Coins

Many Mormons will claim archaeological support for the Book of Mormon and try to place its cities and lands in Central and Middle America.[13] But unlike the Bible, which has much detailed archaeological support, the Book of Mormon *has very little that is officially recognized by the Mormon Church.* Members will claim many things, but there is little or no official recognition of these claims. This was demonstrated in the Mormon teaching manual (*Book of Mormon*, Student Manual Religion 121 and 122, 1989). Page 163 is titled "possible Book of Mormon sites." The title's use of the disclaimer "possible" is reinforced at the bottom of the page with the statement: "No effort should be made to identify points on this map with any existing geographical locations." If Book of Mormon sites (cities and places) were known, this would have been the place to say so.

The reality is that no coins and artifacts and few people, cities, and places identified in the Book of Mormon have ever been officially located by the Mormon Church. Exceptions include Joseph Smith, the City of Manti, and Hill Cumorah (near Palmyra, New York). Hill Cumorah is the place where Joseph Smith allegedly received the gold plates that he allegedly translated into the Book of Mormon and the place where two great extermination battles allegedly took place (Ether 15:2, 11; Mormon 6:9–15; 8:2–3). Joseph Smith had the following to say about the city of Manti:

> The camp passed through Huntsville, in Randolph County [Missouri], which has been appointed as one of the stakes of Zion, and is the ancient site of the city of Manti. . . .[14]

The city of Manti is mentioned in the Book of Mormon. The index of this book under *Manti, land of,* has: "Most southerly land of Nephites"; and under *Manti, city of,* it has: "chief city in land of Manti." All this information then leads to the conclusion that the land of Manti is allegedly in the state of Missouri, in the United States. Mormon historian Apostle Joseph Fielding Smith in his book *Doctrines of Salvation* (3:239–241), reaches the same conclusion. Yet no archaeological evidence has been produced to show that such an ancient city actually existed there.

The fact still remains that there is no archaeological evidence in support of the Book of Mormon officially accepted by the Mormon Church.

Animals, Plants, and Metals

The Book of Mormon in its main story line (roughly 600 B.C. to A.D. 400, which excludes the Book of Ether) speaks of a variety of animals, plants, and metals that existed in the Americas during its time frame:

- Iron: 2 Nephi 5:15; 20:34; Jarom 1:8; Mosiah 11:8.
- Steel: 1 Nephi 4:9; 16:18; 2 Nephi 5:15.
- Asses (donkeys): 1 Nephi 18:25; Mosiah 5:14; 12:5.
- Horses: Alma 18:9; 3 Nephi 3:22 (note that horses were used to pull chariots); 1 Nephi 18:25; Enos 1:21.
- Cattle, cows, oxen: Enos 1:21; 3 Nephi 3:22; 6:1; 1 Nephi 18:25.
- Pig (sow): 3 Nephi 7:8.
- Grain, wheat: Mosiah 9:9; Helaman 11:17.
- Silk: 1 Nephi 13:7; Alma 1:29.

Archaeologists and the prestigious Smithsonian Institution in a letter to John Farkas, reproduced in our book *How to Rescue Your Loved One from Mormonism,* say that the New World had *none* of the principal Old World domesticated food plants or animals (except the dog, which the Book of Mormon mentions only once, in 3 Nephi 7:8). There were no horses (of any size), no elephants, iron, steel, wheat, barley, oats, millet, rice, cattle, pigs, chickens, donkeys (asses), and silk in the New World during the Book of Mormon time frame. There were traces of items made from iron and steel of meteoric origin, but the technology to make steel was not present. The above-listed items did not start to arrive in the New World until the Old World peoples brought them starting around A.D. 1500.

Hundreds of Thousands Die with No Artifacts?

The Book of Mormon says:

> He saw that there had been slain by the sword already nearly **two millions** of his people, and he began to sorrow in his heart; yea, there had been slain **two millions** of mighty men, and also their **wives and their children.** . . . And it came to pass that the army of Coriantumr did pitch their tents by the hill Ramah; and it was that same hill [Hill Cumorah, near Palmyra, New York] where my father Mormon did hide up the records unto the Lord, which were sacred. (Ether 15:2, 11, also see verses 15–30)

These are the pre-Nephite people (the Jaredites) who were just coming to their end with the arrival of the people of the main story line of the Book of Mormon, Lehi and his family, as they arrived from Jerusalem in 600 B.C. The final Jaredite battle allegedly took place on the same Hill Cumorah as the later extermination battle between the Nephites and the Lamanites in A.D. 385.

> And when they had gone through and hewn down all my people **save it were twenty and four of us,** (among whom was my son Moroni) and we having survived the dead of our people, did behold on the morrow, when the Lamanites had returned unto their camps, from the top of the hill Cumorah, the **ten thousand** of my people who were hewn down, being led in the front by me. And we also beheld the **ten thousand** of my people who were led by my son Moroni. And behold, the **ten thousand** of Gidgiddonah had fallen, and he also in the midst. And Lamah had fallen with his **ten thousand**; and Gigal had fallen with his **ten thousand**; and Limhah had fallen with his ten thousand; and Jeneum had fallen

with his **ten thousand**; and Cumenihah, and Moronihah, and Antionum, and Shiblom, and Shem, and Josh, had fallen **with their ten thousand each**. And it came to pass that there were **ten more who did fall by the sword, with their ten thousand each**; yea, even all my people, save it were those twenty and four who were with me, and also a **few** who had **escaped into the south countries**, and a few who had deserted over unto the Lamanites, had fallen; and their flesh, and bones, and blood lay upon the face of the earth, being left by the hands of those who slew them to molder upon the land, and to crumble and to return to their mother earth. (Mormon 6:11–15)

And now it came to pass that after the great and tremendous battle at Cumorah, behold, the Nephites who had **escaped into the country southward** were hunted by the Lamanites, **until they were all destroyed**. And my father also was killed by them, and **I even remain alone** to write the sad tale of the destruction of my people. But behold, they are gone, and I fulfil the commandment of my father. And whether they will slay me, I know not. (Mormon 8:2–3)

This is the extermination battle on Hill Cumorah in A.D. 385 that allegedly killed 240,000 Nephite warriors (not including wives and children, who were also present, Mormon 6:7), and probably the same number of Lamanites. The Book of Ether in the Book of Mormon relates that another great battle took place there hundreds of years earlier (see Ether 15, part of which is quoted above). It seems reasonable to expect that items that would not decay easily, such as arrowheads, stone axeheads, copper, silver, and gold items, gold and silver coins (see Alma chapter 11 heading and 11:4–19) would be found in farming the land and in excavations at the site. Iron and steel would leave their oxides in the form of rust as they decayed. But none of these has been found.

In 1834 Joseph Smith claimed to have found near the bank of the Illinois River (in an Indian mound) the bones of Zelph, a white Lamanite, who was killed in the "last great struggle of the Lamanites and Nephites" (*History of The Church* [June 3, 1834], 2:79–80; *Times and Seasons,* 6:788). So at the very least some bones should also be found. But the reality is that no unusual artifacts have ever been found at or around Hill Cumorah. This is the case even though major construction has taken place on and at the base of the hill. A four-lane road has been built at the base of Hill Cumorah, a paved road was built to the top of the hill, and a visitors' center was constructed part way up the hill—all without encountering the artifacts that would be expected if hundreds of thousands had died there.

A Comparison of Mormon Teachings on the Nature of God

Joseph Smith, the founder and first president of the Mormon Church, said at its April 1844 General Conference: "It is necessary we should understand the character and being of God. . . . It is the first principle of the gospel to know for a certainty the character of God. . . ." Brigham Young, the second president of the Mormon Church, said similarly on February 8, 1857: "It is one of the first principles of the doctrine of salvation to become acquainted with our Father and our God."[15] Tell your Mormon contact that you agree that it is important to know and understand the character of God as taught in the LDS scriptures and teaching manuals.

Mormonism's founder Joseph Smith departed radically from traditional Christianity in his teachings on God:

> God an exalted man—I will go back to the beginning before the world was, to show what kind of being God is. What sort of a being was God in the beginning? . . . I am going to tell you how God came to be God. **We have imagined and supposed that God was God from all eternity. I will refute that idea, and take away the veil, so that you may see.** . . . It is the first principle of the gospel to know for a certainty the character of God. . . . That **he was once a man like us**; yea, that God himself, the father of us all **dwelt on an earth.** . . . (*Teachings of The Prophet Joseph Smith*, pp. 345–46)[16]

Joseph Fielding Smith took this from a talk given by Joseph Smith at an official Mormon Church meeting (General Conferice) in April 1844 known as "The King Follett Discourse." Mormon teaching manuals expand on this doctrine:

> Our Father Advanced and Progressed Until He Became God. President Joseph Fielding Smith said: 'Our Father in heaven according to the prophet [Joseph Smith], had a father, and since there has been a condition of this kind through all eternity, each father had a father' (*Doctrines of Salvation*, 2:47). President Joseph F. Smith taught: "I know that God is a being with body, parts and passions. . . . Man was born of woman; Christ the savior, was born of woman; and God the father was born of woman." (*Church News,* 19 Sept. 1936, p. 2)[17]

> As shown in this chapter, our Father in heaven was once a man as we are now, capable of physical death . . . he and our mother in heaven were empowered to give birth to spirit children. . . .[18]

Mormon Apostle Orson Pratt taught in the periodical *The Seer*:

> We were begotten by our Father in Heaven; the person of our Father in Heaven was begotten on a previous heavenly world by His Father; and again, he was begotten by a still more ancient Father; and so on from generation to generation, from one heavenly world to another more ancient, until our minds are wearied and lost in the multiplicity of generations and successive worlds. . . . (1853, p. 132)

Mormon scripture adds further detail:

> The **Father has a body of flesh and bones as tangible as man's;** the Son also; but the Holy Ghost has not a body of flesh and bones, but is a personage of Spirit. Were it not so, the Holy Ghost could not dwell in us. (D&C 130:22, April, 1843)

Note how the above references say the Father has a body of flesh and bones "as tangible as man's," he was once a man like us, he was born of a woman, he dwelt on an earth, he has not always been God, and he had a father. Now compare these ideas to the following Book of Mormon teaching that the Father is a spirit:

> Holy, holy God; we believe that thou art God, and we believe that thou art holy, and that thou **wast a spirit,** and that **thou art a spirit,** and that thou **wilt be a spirit forever.** (Alma 31:15)[19]

This is not the only Book of Mormon reference about God being a spirit. There are other references (Alma 18:2–5, 26–28; 22:8–11; Mosiah 15:3–5). Couple this with the Doctrine and Covenants 93:21–23 and the very clear Lecture Fifth of Faith, all shown below, and the case is ironclad: the early Mormon scriptures clearly taught that God was a spirit.

Now this was the tradition of Lamoni, which he had received from his father, **that there was a Great Spirit.** Notwithstanding **they believed in a Great Spirit** they supposed that whatsoever they did was right; nevertheless, Lamoni began to fear exceedingly, with fear lest he had done wrong in slaying his servants. . . . And he said, yea. And Ammon said: **This is God.** And Ammon said unto him again: **Believest thou that this Great Spirit, who is God,** created all things which are in heaven and in the earth? (Alma 18:5, 27–28)

And now when Aaron heard this, his heart began to rejoice, and he said: Behold, assuredly as thou livest, O king, there is a God. And the king said: **Is God that Great Spirit** that brought our fathers out of the land of Jerusalem? And Aaron said unto him: **Yea, he is that Great Spirit, and he created all things both in heaven and in earth.** Believest thou this? And he said: Yea, I believe that the Great Spirit created all things, and I desire that ye should tell me concerning all these things, and I will believe thy words. (Alma 22:8–11)

. . . The Father and Son—and **they are one God,** yea, the very Eternal Father of heaven and earth. And thus **the flesh becoming subject to the spirit, <u>or</u> the Son to the Father, being one God.** . . . (Mosiah 15:3–5)

. . . Ye were also in the beginning with **the Father; that which is Spirit,** even the spirit of truth (D&C 93:21–23, May 1833).

There are two personages[20] who constitute the great, matchless, governing and supreme power over all things—by whom all things were created. . . . They are the Father and the Son: **The Father being a personage of spirit,** glory and power: possessing all perfection and fullness: The Son, who was in the bosom of the Father,

a personage of tabernacle [a body]. . . . (1835 D&C, Lecture Fifth
of Faith 5:2, p. 53)[21]

It is not possible to have a body of flesh and bones, as the Mormon God the Father has, and to be a spirit at the same time. Some
Mormons will try to twist this and say, "Yes, God does have a
spirit just as we have a spirit, this is what it really means." But
having a spirit and *being* a spirit are two significantly different
things. They are just as different as: "I am a basketball" or "I have
a basketball." The older Mormon scriptures are very clear in saying "God *is* a spirit."[22]

Contradicting Joseph Smith's teaching that God "was once a
man like us," and the current LDS teaching manuals that agree
with him, are the following LDS scriptures that say the Mormon
God the Father has existed from eternity. (Passages that say the
Son has existed as God from eternity logically require that the
Father has also.)

For behold, the time cometh, and is not far distant, that with
power, the **Lord omnipotent who reigneth, who was, and is from
all eternity to all eternity,** shall come down from heaven among
the children of men, . . . And he shall be called Jesus Christ, the
son of God, the Father of heaven and earth, the Creator of all
things from the beginning; and his mother shall be called Mary.
(Mosiah 3:5, 8)

. . . I, the Lord your God, have created all men. . . . And I do this
that I may prove unto many that **I am the same yesterday, today,
and forever;** and that I speak forth my words according to mine
own pleasure. . . . (2 Nephi 29:7, 9)

By these things we know that there is a **God in heaven, who is
infinite and eternal, from everlasting to everlasting the same
unchangeable God,** the framer of heaven and earth, and all things
which in them are. . . . Which Father, Son, and Holy Ghost are
one God, infinite and eternal, without end. Amen. (D&C 20:17,
28, April 1830)

And God spake unto Moses, saying: Behold, I am the Lord God
almighty, and endless is my name; for **I am without beginning of
days** or end of years; and is not this endless? (Moses 1:3)

From the last four LDS scriptures above, we also learn that God the Father and the Son of God are the same unchangeable God from everlasting to everlasting—he is God without beginning.[23] Yet according to several of the above-quoted LDS teaching manuals, God the Father was once a man with a body of flesh and bones capable of physical death like you and me, and *he progressed to Godhood*. The God of the Bible, on the other hand, has been God from eternity to eternity (Pss. 90:2; 93:2; 103:17; Heb. 13:8).

There is one other major teaching of Mormonism that must now be called to mind. From the following LDS teaching manual we learn that we also can progress to "become Gods like our Heavenly Father":

> **We can become Gods like our Heavenly Father.** This is exaltation . . . BLESSINGS OF EXALTATION . . . These are some of the special blessings given to exalted persons:
>
> 2. They will become Gods.
> 3. They will have their righteous family members with them and will be able to have spirit children also. These spirit children will have the same relationship to them as we do to our Heavenly Father. They will be an eternal family. . . .
> 4. **They will have everything** that our Heavenly Father and Jesus Christ have, all power, glory, dominion, and knowledge. . . . (*Gospel Principles*, p. 290)

In other words, we could also have everything the Father and Son have: "all power, glory, dominion, and knowledge." As Mormon Apostle Orson Pratt expressed, we would be one of a multitude of Gods going back into eternity. In contrast to this, the Bible and the Book of Mormon both teach that there is only one God—and there never will be another. The following Bible verses clearly say there is only one God:

> Ye are my witnesses, saith the LORD,[24] and my servant whom I have chosen: that ye may know and believe me, and understand that I am he: **before me there was no God formed, neither shall there be after me.** (Isa. 43:10)

Thus saith the LORD the King of Israel, and his redeemer the Lord of hosts; I am the first, and I am the last; and beside me there is no God. . . . Fear ye not, neither be afraid: have not I told thee from that time, and have declared it? Ye are even my witnesses. Is there a God beside me? Yea, there is no God; I know not any. (Isa. 44:6, 8)

Thus saith the LORD, thy redeemer, and he that formed thee from the womb, I am the LORD that maketh all things; that stretcheth forth the heavens **alone**; that spreadeth abroad the earth **by myself**.[25] (Isa. 44:24)

I am the LORD, and **there is none else, there is no God beside me:** I girded thee, though thou hast not known me: that they may know from the rising of the sun, and from the west, that there is none beside me. **I am the LORD, and there is none else.** (Isa. 45:5–6)

Tell ye, and bring them near; yea, let them take counsel together: who hath declared this from ancient time? who hath told it from that time? have not I the LORD? and **there is no God else beside me;** a just God and **a Saviour; there is none beside me.** (Isa. 45:5–6, 21)

For when God made promise to Abraham, because he could swear by no greater, he sware by himself. (Heb. 6:13)

Unto thee it was showed, that thou mightest know that the LORD he is God; there is none else beside him. (Deut. 4:35)

The following Book of Mormon verses also say there is only one God:

Now Zeezrom said: Is there more than one God? And he answered, No. . . . Now Zeezrom saith again unto him: Is the Son of God the very Eternal Father? And Amulek said unto him: Yea, he is the very Eternal Father . . . shall be brought and be arraigned before the bar of Christ the Son, and God the father, and the Holy Spirit, **which is one Eternal God. . . .** (Alma 11:28–29, 38–39, 44)

. . . Unto the father, and unto the Son, and unto the Holy Ghost, **which are one God. . . .** (Mormon 7:7)

. . . But there is **no God beside me. . . .** (Moses 1:6)

To explain these, some Mormons might say, "They only mean 'One God in purpose.'" There is no Mormon Scripture that clearly supports this idea. They may also say that Isaiah 44:6, 8 is only talking about idols. It is correct that Isaiah 44 is partially about idols, but at the same time the context makes it clear that it also precludes the existence of any other God, even a supposed father of God the Father. Another usual response is "God (and/or Jesus Christ) is the God of this earth only—of only this world. This is why the verses say there is only one God, no other Gods." The following verses make it clear that God is the God of *all* creation, not just of this world only, but of the whole universe:[26]

> Thou, even thou, art LORD alone; thou hast made heaven, the heaven of heavens, with all their host, the earth, and all things that are therein, the seas, and all that is therein, and thou preservest them all; and the host of heaven worshippeth thee. (Neh. 9:6)

> For by him were all things created, that are in heaven, and that are in earth, visible and invisible, whether they be thrones, or dominions, or principalities, or powers: all things were created by him, and for him. (Col. 1:16)

> Hath in these last days spoken unto us by his Son, whom he hath appointed heir of all things, by whom also **he made the worlds;** (Heb. 1:2)

> And **worlds without number have I created;** and I also created them for mine own purpose; and by the son I created them, which is mine only begotten. . . . For behold, there are **many worlds that have passed away** by the word of my power. And there are many that now stand, and innumerable are they unto man. . . . (Moses 1:33, 35)

> That **by him . . . the worlds are and were created,** and the inhabitants thereof are begotten sons and daughters unto God. (D&C 76:24)

It is reasonable to ask: When did the Mormon descriptions of God change? Why is there a difference between the various LDS sources? The answer is found in the quote of Joseph Smith at the beginning of this chapter from his "King Follett Discourse" (April 1844). President Smith publicly introduced at this time a significant change in LDS doctrine when he said: "We have imagined and supposed that God was God from all eternity. I will refute that idea, and take away the veil, so you may see." Earlier, in Doctrine and Covenants 130:22[27] (April 1843) there was another significant change: God the father now had a body of flesh and bones instead of being a spirit. These *newer* Mormon teachings are indeed in conflict with the *older* LDS scriptures and with the Bible, but most of the *older* LDS teachings have never been removed. The teachings are all supposed to be correct and compatible, but this is not logically possible. God cannot have a body of flesh and bones and at the same time be a spirit. He cannot be the one and only God from everlasting to everlasting and at the same time be just one among many who progress to become Gods.

How could Joseph Smith be a true prophet of God and yet proclaim conflicting teachings on the attributes of God? What confidence can we have in him and his other teachings if he could make such a gross mistake about such a critical item?

Having a proper description of the attributes of God was very important to Joseph Smith (and it should be to us also!).[28] At the same meeting where he said, "We have imagined and supposed that God was God from all eternity. I will refute that idea, and take away the veil, so that you may see," he also said, "it is the first principle[29] of the gospel to know for a certainty the character of God. . . ." (*Teachings of the Prophet Joseph Smith*, p. 345). Did Joseph Smith truly know the character of God? It is very important to know the character of God, and we should reject descriptions of God that conflict with what he reveals about himself in the Bible. The first commandment says, "Thou shalt have no other Gods before me" (Exod. 20:3). Joseph Smith broke this commandment in his "King Follett Discourse." This error has since been incorporated into present-day LDS teaching manuals. In view of these major changes in LDS teachings, can anyone have any confidence in what is now being taught by the Mormon Church?

After exposing Mormonism's contradictions, make sure you do not leave the person you are witnessing to with the feeling that God is unknowable. Encourage him or her to get to know the God of the Bible—that he is the God of the universe, the only God, and that he has been God from eternity. Explain that we can know him when we accept Jesus Christ as our Lord and Savior, and that we can grow in our knowledge of God by regularly reading the Bible.

The Attributes of the Mormon Jesus Christ

Before going on, it is worth recapping what the Mormon Church has taught about the father of Jesus Christ, and to restate what the Bible teaches on the same subject.

According to the teachings of the Mormon Church, the father of Jesus Christ, God the Father, now has a body of flesh and bones. He has not been God from all eternity; he was once a man like you and me; he has a father and progressed to become a God. (This implies that God the Father has a spirit and body that must also have been procreated just like ours and Christ's were.)

The Bible tells us that God the Father has always been God in eternity past; he never, ever was a man that progressed to become a God. The Bible is clear that there is only one God, the Lord, who knows everything and would not lie to us, knows nothing about his having ancestors (a father, grandfather, great grandfather, and so on). The Bible says God the Father *is* a spirit.

The Mormon Church has significant nonbiblical teachings about Jesus Christ. It teaches that the body of Jesus Christ was procreated in the same way we men and women were procreated by our parents. This is illustrated by the following from LDS leaders and teaching manuals:

Christ is the only begotten (Moses 1:6, 17, 21, 33; 2:1, 26–27; 3:18; 4:1), the Only Begotten Son (Jacob. 4:5, 11; Alma 12:33–34; 13:5; D&C 20:21; 29:42; 49:5; 76:13, 25; John 1:18; 3:16), the Only Begotten of the Father. (Moses 5:9.) These name-titles all

signify that **our Lord is the only Son of the Father in the flesh.**
Each of the words is to be **understood literally.** Only means only;
begotten means begotten; and son means son. **Christ was begotten by an immortal father in the same way that mortal men are
begotten by mortal fathers.** (Apostle Bruce R. McConkie)[30]

God the Father is a perfected, glorified, holy man, an immortal
personage. And Christ was born into the world as the **Literal Son
of this Holy Being;** he was born in the same personal, real, and
literal sense that any mortal son is born to a mortal father. There
is **nothing figurative about his paternity;** he was **begotten, conceived and born in the normal and natural course of events,** for
he is the Son of God, and that designation means what it says.
(1 Ne. 11.). (Apostle Bruce R. McConkie)[31]

We first begin to read that Jesus came in the flesh. . . . But suppose I examine that, a moment. The new testament tells me that
the Father gave His only-begotten Son a ransom for the sins of
the world. Do you believe that, brother B.? Do you believe that
Jesus Christ is the only-begotten son of the father? "yes." Do you
believe the Son was begotten by the Father, as the Apostles said
he was? **Here I shall have to disagree with you,** to begin with; for
I believe the Father came down from heaven, as the Apostles said
he did, and begot the Saviour of the world; **for he is the ONLY-
begotten of the Father, which could not be if the Father did not
actually beget him in person.** (Brigham Young) July 24, 1853,
Journal of Discourses, 1:237–238)

A MODERN PROPHET'S ANSWER . . . I want the little folks
[children] to hear what I am going to tell you. I am going to tell
you a **simple truth,** yet it is one of the **greatest truths** and one of
the most **simple facts ever revealed** to the children of men.
You all know that your fathers are indeed your fathers and that
your mothers are indeed your mothers—you all know that don't
you? You can not deny it. Now, we are told in scriptures that Jesus
Christ is the only begotten Son of God in the flesh. **Well, now for
the benefit of the older ones, how are children begotten? I answer
just as Jesus Christ was begotten of his father.** . . . Now my little
friends, I will repeat again in words as simple as I can, and you
talk to your parents about it, that God, the eternal father, **is literally the father of Jesus Christ.** (Joseph F. Smith)[32]

... he was *able* to make payment because he lived a sinless life and because **he was actually, literally, biologically the Son of God in the flesh.** *(Messages For Exaltation)*[33]

In contrast, the Bible in Matthew 1:20 and Luke 1:35 says that the Holy Ghost overshadowed Mary. The only conclusion is that it was a miraculous event, not a physical one.

Is Jesus Christ Married?

Top leaders of the Mormon Church in the mid–1800s taught that Jesus Christ was married. Note, for example, these authoritative teachings by LDS apostles:

I discover that some of the Eastern papers represent me as a great blasphemer, because I said, in my lecture on Marriage, at our last conference, that Jesus Christ was married at Cana [sic] of Galilee, that Mary, Martha, and others were his wives, and that he begat [sic] children. (Apostle Orson Hyde, March 18, 1855)[34]

It will be borne in mind that once on a time, there was a marriage in Cana [sic] of Galilee; and on a careful reading of that transaction, it will be discovered that no less a person than Jesus Christ was married on that occasion. If he was never married, his intimacy with Mary and Martha, and the other Mary also whom Jesus loved, must have been highly unbecoming and improper to say the best of it. (Orson Hyde, no date given)[35]

The grand reason of the burst of public sentiment in Anathemas upon Christ and his disciples, causing his crucifixion, was evidently based upon polygamy, according to the testimony of the philosophers who rose in that age. A belief in the doctrine of a plurality of wives caused the persecution of Jesus and his followers. We might almost think they were "Mormons." (Jedediah M. Grant, August 7, 1853)[36]

Next let us enquire whether there are any intimations in Scripture concerning the wives of Jesus ... it is necessary that He should have one or more wives by whom He could multiply His seed. ...
If all the acts of Jesus were written, we no doubt should learn that

these beloved women [Mary, Martha, and Mary Magdalene] were his wives. . . . (Apostle Orson Pratt, October 1853)[37]

Modern Mormon literature is surprisingly quiet on this subject. The earlier teachings about Christ's being married are neither restated nor denied. Current LDS instructional manuals simply maintain silence on the issue, although they do state that God the Father is married to a mother in heaven:

> Our father in heaven lives in an exalted marriage relationship "No matter to what heights God has attained or may attain, he does not stand alone; for side by side with him, in all her glory, a glory like unto his, stands a companion, the mother of his children. For as we have a father in heaven, so also we have a mother there, a glorified, exalted, ennobled mother." . . . As shown in this chapter, our Father in heaven was once a man as we are now, capable of physical death . . . he progressed from one stage of life to another until he attained the state that we call exaltation or Godhood. In such a condition, he and our mother in heaven were empowered to give birth to spirit children. . . . (*Achieving A Celestial Marriage*, pp. 129, 132)

> Man, as a spirit, was begotten and born of heavenly parents. . . . The first spirit born to our heavenly parents was Jesus Christ. . . . We can become Gods like our heavenly father. This is exaltation. . . . They [couples] will become Gods. . . . And will be able to have spirit children also. These spirit children will have the same relationship to them as we do to our Heavenly Father. They will be an eternal family. . . . (*Gospel Principles*, 1986 edition or older, pp. 9, 290)

Mormon teachings also present as a prerequisite for *any* man to attain exaltation and thus become a God, that he must first be married for time and eternity:

> Remarks of the Prophet [Joseph Smith] at Ramus [May 1843] . . . Except a man and his wife enter into **an everlasting covenant** and be married for eternity, while in this probation, by the power and authority of the Holy Priesthood, **they will cease to increase when they die; that is, they will not have any children after the resur-**

rection. But those who are married by the power and authority of the priesthood in this life, and continue without committing the sin against the Holy Ghost, will continue to increase and have children in the celestial glory. (*Teachings of the Prophet Joseph Smith*, pp. 300–301; *History of the Church*, 5:391)

In the celestial glory there are three heavens or degrees; and in order to obtain the highest, a man must enter into this order of the priesthood [meaning the new and everlasting covenant of marriage].[38] (D&C 131:1–2)

And again, verily I say unto you, . . . And if it be after the first resurrection, in the next resurrection; and shall inherit thrones, kingdoms, principalities, and powers, dominions, all heights and depths—then shall it be written in the Lamb's Book of Life, that he shall commit no murder whereby to shed innocent blood, and if ye abide in my covenant, and commit no murder whereby to shed innocent blood, it shall be done unto them in all things whatsoever my servant hath put upon them, in time, and through all eternity; and shall be of full force when they are out of the world; and they shall pass by the angels, and the Gods, which are set there, **to their exaltation and glory** in all things, as hath been sealed upon their heads, which glory shall be a fullness and a continuation of the seeds forever and ever. (D&C 132:19)

4. We must be married for time and eternity. *(Gospel Principles)*[39]

Since the Bible says nothing to indicate that Christ was married during his earthly ministry, Mormon teachings on this subject furnish grounds for new Mormons or potential converts to reexamine what sort of sect they are getting into.

Table 1-A Reference Summary—Mormon Sources
Attributes of God the Father in the references listed

Reference	Always God from eternity	Not from eternity	Once a man like us	Progressed to godhood	Is a spirit	Has body of flesh & bones	Has a father
Mormon Sources:							
J. Smith, pp. 345, 373	no	yes	yes	yes		yes	yes
Search, p. 152	no	yes	yes	yes		yes	yes
Achieving, pp. 129–132	no	yes	yes	yes		yes	yes
D&C 130:22						yes	
Alma 31:15					yes		
Mosiah 15:3–5					yes		
D&C 93:21–23					yes		
Lecture Fifth					yes		
Mosiah 3:5, 8	yes						
2 Nep 29:7, 9	yes						
D&C 20:17, 28	yes						
Moses 1:3	yes						

Code: J. Smith = Teachings of the Prophet Joseph Smith; Search = Search These Commandments; Achieving = Achieving a Celestial Marriage

Table 1-B Reference Summary—Biblical References
Attributes of God the Father in the references listed

Reference	Always God from eternity, only one God	Not from eternity	Once a man like us	Progressed to godhood	God not man	God is a spirit
Biblical References:						
Isaiah 43:10	yes					
44:6, 8	yes					
44:24	yes					
45:5–6, 21	yes					
Psalms 90:2	yes					
93:2	yes					
103:17	yes					
Deuteronomy 4:35	yes					
33:27	yes					
Nehemiah 9:6	yes					
Hosea 11:9					yes	
Numbers 23:19					yes	
John 4:24						yes
Hebrews 6:13	yes					

4

For Non-Mormons and Mormons

The subjects presented here are generally best covered with the Mormon who seems[1] familiar with the history and unique teachings of the Mormon Church. They may also be used with those who have little background in Mormonism, but such individuals may have difficulty understanding the full significance of what is said. The first discussion deals with discrepancies between the Mormon scriptures or *standard works* and current LDS teachings, whereas the second focuses on failed Mormon prophecies of Christ's second coming.

Are There Major Mormon Church Teachings Not Found in the *Standard Works?*

When challenged concerning the teachings of their church, Mormons frequently dismiss evidence of contradictions or error by saying, "We can reject a teaching from anyone or any Mormon leader if it is not in the *standard works*. It is just their opinion, and I do not have to be concerned about it." Is this correct?

56

No, it is not. The LDS Church says the instructions of the President of the Church are "more than the advice of man," "from the Lord," "the mind of the Lord, the will of the Lord . . . unto salvation," "scripture to us." In summary, "When our leaders speak, the thinking has been done." (Appendix 4 has more information on this subject.) Actual LDS practice shows that these statements have been followed. It is important to understand and keep this idea in mind as you study the examples below and discuss them with Mormons who will try to hide behind the *standard works*.

There are many examples of significant and important teachings of the Mormon Church that have no support at all, or at first had no support, from the *standard works*. In some significant cases, the *standard works* actually speak against the teachings. Note the following examples.

Joseph Smith's King Follett Address

As detailed in chapter 3, we again quote Joseph Smith from his April 1844 King Follett Address:

> God himself was once as we are now, and is an exalted man . . . we have imagined and supposed that God was God from all eternity. I will refute that idea and take away the veil, so that you may see.[2]

Keep in mind that this talk by the founder of the Mormon Church was given at an official LDS Church meeting, a General Conference. Joseph Smith's King Follett Address was accepted even though the Mormon Church since its 1835 Doctrine and Covenants and the 1830 Book of Mormon[3] said God was God from eternity to eternity.

There may seem to be some connection between Smith's King Follett Address and an April 1843 revelation (D&C 130:22) that says the Father has a body of flesh and bones. However, even though this revelation is dated April 1843, it does not appear that it was made available to the LDS general membership of the period. It was not included in the Doctrine and Covenants until the 1876 edition and was not accepted by the membership until the October 1880 General Conference.[4] Thus, from 1876 onward, Doctrine and Covenants 130:22 said, "The Father has a body of flesh and bones," whereas other passages in the Doctrine and Covenants and the Book of Mormon said God was a spirit.[5] This internal contradiction continued until the 1921 edition of the Doctrine and Covenants when the *Lectures on Faith* were excluded. The Book of Mormon references and what is now Doctrine and Covenants 20:12, 17, 28 were unchanged and continue to contradict current LDS teachings on God's origin and his allegedly having a body of flesh and bones.

Polygamy

An example of a doctrine at first not based on the *standard works* is the teaching and practice of polygamy (actually polygyny); that is, that Mormon men could have more than one wife. Polygamy was practiced from about 1835 to about 1905. Yet the 1835 Doctrine and Covenants in Section 101:4, titled "Marriage," said: "In asmuch [sic] as this church of Christ has been reproached with the crime of fornication, and polygamy: we declare that we believe, that one man should have one wife; and one woman but one husband except in case of death . . ." (p. 251). This verse continued to appear in Mormon scripture until it was excluded from the 1876 edition of the Doctrine and Covenants. Doctrine and Covenants, 132, which allowed the practice of polygamy, was allegedly received in 1843, but was not publicly announced until August 29, 1852, and was not voted on until October 1880. So the practice preceded by decades its supposed basis in Mormon scripture. In addition, the practice of polygamy did not end in 1890 with the membership approval of "Official Declaration—1." This was supposed to officially end the practice, but in reality it continued in private with official sanction for about another fifteen years while at the same time it was publicly denied.[6]

Temple Ceremonies

The sacred Mormon temple ceremonies are another example of major doctrine not based on the *standard works*. These ceremonies are so sacred that most Mormons will not talk about them in any depth, and many will not discuss them at all. Most of the temple activities are based on the Mormon Church's teaching that sacred ordinances (baptism, laying on of hands to receive the Holy Ghost, male ordination to the priesthood, marriage for time and eternity) performed for the living must also be done on earth for those who have died without having an opportunity to receive them.

The concept of proxy work for the dead is found in Doctrine and Covenants 128, 137 (Alvin mentioned there died before the start of the Mormon Church), and 138, but details and wording of the present LDS temple ceremonies are not found there. In fact, Doctrine and Covenants 137 seems to rule out any need for such ceremonies; it declares that people would be heirs of the celestial kingdom of God if they died without the requisite knowledge but "would have received it if they had been permitted to tarry [remain alive longer]." Interestingly, although Doctrine and Covenants 26:2 and 28:13 require that "all things shall be done by common consent in the church," LDS leaders changed the temple endowment ceremony in April 1990 without a show of hands (membership approval). There is more on this subject below under "Proxy Work for the Dead."

Mother in Heaven

A fourth example is the LDS teaching about a mother in heaven, the nameless wife of God the Father. While this is a basic LDS belief taught in their teaching manuals,[7] it is not found in any Mormon scripture.

Three Gods, But One God in Purpose

The fifth example is found in the Mormon Church's teaching that the Father, the Son, and the Holy Ghost are separate and distinct entities—three Gods[8]—who are one God in purpose. The LDS Church uses the term "one in purpose" to sidestep the accusation of being tritheistic[9] (three Gods), not monotheistic (one God). The clear teaching that they are "one God in purpose"[10] is not stated in any Mormon scripture. Yet LDS members state this frequently on the basis of their other books and teaching manuals.

Elohim and Jehovah

Our sixth example is the LDS teaching about the names and separate identities of their Gods. Since Joseph Smith at the April 1844 General Conference said ". . . it is necessary we should understand the character and being of God. . . . It is the first principle of the Gospel to know for a certainty the Character of God . . ."[11] it seems reasonable to expect a correct understanding of God to be clearly taught. (However, we have already noted confusion in the first and fifth examples above.) Related to this is the LDS teaching that *Elohim* is God the Father and *Jehovah* is the name of the pre-incarnate Jesus Christ—a teaching of the Mormon Church[12] that is not clearly stated in Mormon scripture. In fact, LDS scriptures are very confusing on this subject. For example, in the Book of Mormon, 2 Nephi 26:12; Mosiah 7:27; 15:1–5; 16:15; Alma 11:38.39; and Ether 3:14 all say the Son is both the *Eternal Father* and the Son, the *Eternal God, Mighty God, Everlasting Father.* The Book of Abraham 2:7–8 and 3:18–19, 22, 27 say Jehovah is God the Father; he is the most intelligent of all spirits; and (in 3:27) he sent the Son of Man (Jesus Christ).

There was so much confusion in Mormonism at the turn of this century that the First Presidency with the Twelve Apostles on June 30, 1916, published a position paper stating that Elohim is God the Father and Jehovah is the pre-incarnate Jesus Christ.[13] This gave the LDS Church a clear position on the matter—a position that remains at odds with verses such as Deuteronomy 6:4; 4:35, 39; 7:9; and 1 Kings 18:39, which in Hebrew identify *Jehovah* as *Elohim*.

Blood Atonement

Brigham Young, the second LDS President and Prophet, taught that there were some sins a person could commit, that required their own blood be shed to be forgiven. This is called *blood atonement*. Several recent LDS leaders have said it was not practiced. One LDS leader said anti-Mormons used parts of talks by Mr. Young to wrongly accuse him of something he did not practice, but did teach. Apostle Bruce R. McConkie says:

> From the days of Joseph Smith to the present, wicked and evilly-disposed persons have fabricated false and slanderous stories to the effect that the Church, in the early days of this dispensation, engaged in a practice of blood atonement whereunder the blood of apostates and others was shed by the Church as an atonement for their sins. **These claims are false and were known by their originators to be false. There is not one historical instance of so-called blood atonement in this dispensation,** nor has there been one event or occurrence whatever, of any nature, from which the slightest inference arises that any such practice either existed or was taught . . . dishonest persons have attempted to make it appear that Brigham Young and others taught things just the opposite of what they really believed and taught. (*Mormon Doctrine*, p. 92)

But then Mr. McConkie goes on to admit that some sins cannot be forgiven:

> But under certain circumstances there are some serious sins for which the cleansing of Christ does not operate, and the law of God is that men must then have their own blood shed to atone for their sins. Murder, for instance, is one of these sins; hence we find the Lord commanding capital punishment. (*Mormon Doctrine*, p. 92)

The Doctrine and Covenants also supports the above:

> And now, behold, I speak unto the church. Thou shalt not kill; and he that kills shall not have forgiveness in this world, nor in the world to come. (D&C 42:18)

However, Brigham Young *did* teach and allow the practice of blood atonement, as can be seen from the following:

There are sins that men commit for which they cannot receive forgiveness in this world, or in that which is to come, and if they had their eyes open to see their true condition, they would be perfectly willing to have their blood spilt upon the ground, that the smoke thereof might ascend to heaven as an offering for their sins; and the smoking incense would atone for their sins, whereas, if such is not the case, they will stick to them and remain upon them in the spirit world . . . I know that there are transgressors, who, if they knew themselves, and the only condition upon which they can obtain forgiveness would beg of their brethren to shed their blood, that the smoke thereof might ascend to God. . . . It is true that the blood of the Son of God was shed for sins through the fall and those committed by men, yet men can commit sins which it can never remit. . . . (President Brigham Young, Sept. 21, 1856)[14]

Suppose you found your brother in bed with your wife, and put a javelin through both of them, you would be justified, **and they would atone for their sins, and be received into the kingdom of God.** I would at once do so in such a case; and under such circumstances, I have no wife whom I love so well that I would not put a javelin through her heart, and I would do it with clean hands. (President Brigham Young, March 16, 1856)[15]

I could refer you to plenty of instances where men have been righteously slain, in order to atone for their sins. I have seen scores and hundreds of people for whom there would have been a chance (in the last resurrection there will be) if their lives had been taken and their blood spilled on the ground as a smoking incense to the Almighty, but who are now angels to the devil, until our elder brother Jesus Christ raises them up—conquers death, hell, and the grave. I have known a great many men who have left this Church for whom there is no chance whatever for exaltation, **but if their blood had been spilled, it would have been better for them.** (President Brigham Young, February 8, 1857)[16]

Was blood atonement actually practiced? Yes, the above quote from Brigham Young shows that. And there is other evidence, but details are too complicated to include here.[17] The Mountain Meadows Massacre in 1857, where about 120 non-Mormon men, women, and children were slaughtered by Mormons and Indians, clearly shows that Mormonism, in Brigham Young's time, led men to do terrible things in the name of God.

The Bible teaches us that the sincere repentant sinner, who has Jesus Christ as Lord and Savior, is forgiven of *all* sin (1 John 1:7). That LDS leaders would teach otherwise is an indictment of their prophetic skills and evidence that they are not called by the one true God of the Bible.

Adam-God Doctrine

Adam-God doctrine is one of the strangest teachings to come out of Mormonism. Brigham Young, the second President and Prophet of the Mormon Church, taught for over twenty years that Adam of the garden of Eden, the Adam of Genesis chapters 1 to 5, is our God the Father, the father of our spirits and the spirit of Jesus Christ, and the literal father of Jesus' body. Many Mormons know very little about this subject. Most who do know it, call it the *Adam-God theory.* One Mormon prophet (Spencer Kimball) said it was "allegedly taught" and called it "false doctrine."[18] He is correct that it is false doctrine, but wrong in claiming it was never taught. Two examples should illustrate what Brigham Young taught many times:

> When our father Adam came into the garden of Eden, he came into it with a celestial body, and brought Eve, one of his wives, with him. He helped to make and organize this world. He is Michael, the Archangel, the Ancient of Days! about whom holy men have written and spoken—He is our Father and our God, and the only God with whom we have to do. (Brigham Young, April 9, 1852)[19]

Note that Young said Adam entered the garden of Eden in a *celestial body.* In LDS terminology a *celestial body* is a resurrected body, and resurrection is one of the events required to reach exaltation:

> Jesus Christ's body was put in the sepulcher a natural body; it was raised a spiritual body. It was placed there in weakness; it

was raised in strength. It was a mortal body when placed in the sepulcher; but when it came forth quickened by spirit, it was no longer a natural or mortal body, it was a spiritual and an immortal body; and with that immortal body he ascended from the earth. . . . But this body was a glorious body, 'the glorious body of the son of god,' and it was in the fashion and likeness of the glorious body of his eternal father. It was a **celestial body** quickened by the celestial glory. And if we wish to attain to the heavenly kingdom we must walk in the ways of life, and sanctify ourselves before God, as Jesus did, so that the influence and power of the celestial kingdom can be with us. (Charles W. Penrose, November 16, 1884)[20]

It was in such a celestial body—which Mormons believe Christ received only upon resurrection—that Adam entered the garden of Eden. Brigham Young taught that Adam was such a resurrected and exalted being—a God, our God:

How much unbelief exists in the minds of latter-day saints in regard to one particular **doctrine which I revealed to them, and which God revealed to me**—namely that Adam is our father and God . . . "Well" says one, "Why was Adam called Adam?" He was the first man on the earth, and its framer and maker . . . Then he said, "I want my children who are in the spirit world to come and live here. I once dwelt upon an earth something like this, in a mortal state. I was faithful. I received my crown and exaltation. . . . I want my children that were born to me in the spirit world to come here and take tabernacles of flesh that their spirits may have a house, a tabernacle. . . ." (Brigham Young,[21] page 308; *Deseret Evening News*, June 14, 1873)

Although Adam-God doctrine has not been officially taught since the turn of the century, the average Mormon today is unaware that it ever was. More knowledgeable members may offer the standard response that the teaching was a personal "theory" of Young rather than a doctrine, or they may imply that it was made up largely by enemies attempting to discredit the LDS Church.

The above quotes may be sufficient to alert a prospective convert; however, before attempting to present the facts to a Mormon, you would do well to show the documentation provided in our book *How to Rescue Your Loved One from Mormonism* (pp. 145–158) and to review the scriptural discussion in our book *Mormons Answered Verse by Verse* (pp. 59–63). These will equip you to prove that Young actually taught that Adam was God and to show that the basis for such a deviant doctrine is still found in the unique LDS scriptures.[22]

Pay for God's Workers

Many Mormons take pride in the fact that the local leaders of their church do not receive pay or salary. In addition, they condemn clergy who do take pay for church work, as Protestants do. Many Mormons do not know that their own top leaders and many others in the hierarchy are also paid. They do not know the facts about current practice, historical practice, and what the Bible says about pay.

The Bible is clear that it is acceptable to take pay for God's work (1 Cor. 9:1–14; 2 Cor. 11:7–9; Num. 18:21; 3 John 1:5–8; Matt. 10:9–10; 1 Tim. 5:17–18; 2 Thess. 3:7–9). Mormons usually take 1 Peter 5:2 and Isaiah 45:13 out of context to defend their position. In the light of all the other verses saying pay is acceptable, these verses need to be interpreted in the context of their own special situation. The following references also show that pay was and still is acceptable in the Mormon Church: Doctrine and Covenants 24:18–19; 42:70–73; 51:13–14; 75:24–25; 84:78–79, 86–89; 119:1–2. The current practice in the Mormon Church is to pay their high-level leaders, teachers, and professors at their schools, and in the church educational system to pay custodians, office workers, and similar.[23]

False Prophecy, Changes, and Contradictions

You may be able to open the way to effective witnessing by first shaking a Mormon's confidence in the LDS Church through documentation of false prophecies, changes, and contradictions. First, though, it is important to highlight accepted Mormon standards for examining these. A past Mormon leader suggested that if Joseph Smith's teachings were built upon fraud and deceit, many errors and contradictions would be easy to detect.

> If Joseph Smith was a deceiver, . . . then he should be exposed; his claims should be refuted, and his doctrines shown to be false, . . . **If his claims and declarations were built upon fraud and deceit, there would appear many errors and contradictions, which would be easy to detect.** The doctrines of false teachers will not stand the test when tried by the accepted standards of measurement, the scriptures. (Apostle Joseph Fielding Smith, 1954)[24]

Significant claims are made by LDS scriptures. Some helpful ones to keep in mind in your discussion with a Mormon are quoted below. But first it should be noted that when presented with false prophecy and contradictions in their scriptures, many Mormons will say something like: "The Bible has false prophecy and contradictions." The implication is that if the Bible can have problems (which it does not) then it is okay for the LDS scriptures to have them. Your best response is to cite the following scriptures that demonstrate the claims of Mormonism about itself. These claims set a very high standard, and Mormons should not be allowed to wriggle free from the obligation to measure Mormonism by that standard. You should ask: "Why would you want to use the Bible as a standard of comparison? Mormonism says the Bible is incomplete and full of errors." (See chapter 6, under "Is the Bible Reliable According to the Mormon Church?" and at the start of chapter 3, "Why the Bible Is Reliable.") Mormons should be held to the standard their leaders and scriptures established.

> And also those to whom these commandments were given, might have power to lay the foundation of this church, and to bring it forth out of obscurity and out of darkness, **the only true and living church upon the face of the whole** earth, with which I, the lord, am well pleased, speaking unto the church collectively and not individually. (D&C 1:30)

Search these commandments, **for they are true and faithful,** and the prophecies and promises which are in them shall all be fulfilled. (D&C 1:37)

For God doth not walk in crooked paths, neither doth he turn to the right hand nor to the left, **neither doth he vary from that which he hath said,** therefore his paths are straight, and his course is one eternal round. (D&C 3:2)

I perceive that it has been made known unto you, by the testimony of his word, that he cannot walk in crooked paths; neither doth he vary from that which he hath said; neither hath he a shadow of turning from the right to the left, or from that which is right to that which is wrong; therefore, his course is one eternal round. (Alma 7:20)

Now, the decrees of God are unalterable; therefore, the way is prepared that whosoever will may walk therein and be saved. (Alma 41:8)

For do we not read that God is the same yesterday, today, and forever, and **in him there is no variableness neither shadow of changing?** And now if ye have imagined up unto yourselves a God who doth vary, and in whom there is shadow of changing, then have ye imagined up unto yourselves a God who is not a God of miracles. (Mormon 9:9–10)

These last three, from the Book of Mormon, have been in LDS scripture since 1830 and those in the Doctrine and Covenants from shortly after the Mormon Church's founding. According to these LDS scriptures, we should find no change or variableness in God's one true church, and the alleged revelations should prove true and faithful.

Moreover, the doctrine and teachings of Joseph Smith are true and without error according to the following:

President Joseph Smith again arose and said—. . . Why do not my enemies strike a blow at the doctrine? They cannot do it, it is truth, and I defy all men to upset it. I am the voice of one crying in the wilderness. (*History of the Church,* 6:273)

When did I [Joseph Smith] ever teach anything wrong from this stand? When was I ever confounded? I want to triumph in Israel before I depart hence and am no more seen. I never told you I was perfect; **but there is no error in the revelations which I have taught.** Must I, then, be thrown away as a thing of naught? (*Teachings of the Prophet Joseph Smith*, p. 368)

(More on the alleged importance of following top leaders of the Mormon Church can be found in appendix 4.)

After establishing these standards, you are ready to examine LDS contradictions and false prophecy. A small sampling is presented here. For more of them, see our book *Mormonism— Changes, Contradictions and Errors.*

Is the Holy Ghost the Only Begotten?

And in that day **the Holy Ghost fell upon Adam, which beareth record of the Father and the Son, saying: I am the Only Begotten of the Father** from the beginning, henceforth and forever, that as thou hast fallen thou mayest be redeemed, and all mankind, even as many as will. (Moses 5:9)

In the Mormon Church, the Only Begotten of the Father is Jesus Christ (*Mormon Doctrine*, p. 546), not the Holy Ghost.

Are Men Baptized after They Have the Priesthood?

And now I speak concerning baptism. Behold, elders, priests, and teachers were baptized; and they were not baptized save they brought forth fruit meet that they were worthy of it. (Moroni 6:1)

In the present LDS Church, Mormon men must be baptized before they obtain the priesthood (*Mormon Doctrine*, pp. 70 and 594).

When May a Person Receive the Holy Ghost—before or after Baptism?

And the morrow after they entered into Caesarea. And Cornelius waited for them, and had called together his kinsmen and near friends. . . . While Peter yet spake these words, **the Holy Ghost fell on all them which heard the word.** And they of the circumcision which believed were astonished, as many as came with Peter, because that on the gentiles also was poured out the gift of the Holy Ghost. For they heard them speak with tongues, and magnify God. Then answered Peter, **Can any man forbid water, that these should not be baptized, which have received the Holy Ghost as well as we?** And he commanded them to be baptized in the name of the Lord. Then prayed they him to tarry certain days. (Acts 10:24, 44–47)

The Mormon Church requires that persons be baptized *before* they have hands laid on them to receive the Holy Ghost (*Mormon Doctrine*, p. 438).

Is Baptism Necessary for Remission of Sins?

. . . Yea, blessed are they who shall believe in your words, and come down into the depths of humility **and be baptized,** for they shall be visited with fire and with the Holy Ghost, **and shall receive a remission of their sins.** (3 Nephi 12:2)

. . . Behold, baptism is unto repentance to the fulfilling the commandments **unto the remission of sins.** (Moroni 8:11)

And again, by way of commandment to the church concerning the manner of baptism—all those who humble themselves before God, and desire to be baptized, and come forth with broken hearts and contrite spirits, and witness before the church that they have truly repented of all their sins, and are willing to take upon them the name of Jesus Christ, having a determination to serve him to the end, **and truly manifest by their works that they have received of the spirit of Christ unto the remission of their sins, shall be received by baptism into his church.** (D&C 20:37)

In this last verse, note that baptism occurs after remission of sins, not before. It seems that, based upon these LDS scriptures, we cannot be sure when it happens. It is the present LDS teaching that remission of sins occurs as a result of repentance and baptism (*Mormon Doctrine*, p. 292).

The Civil War Prophecy

Joseph Smith's alleged Civil War prophecy (Dec. 25, 1832) is often used by Mormons to demonstrate his prophetic skills. But a close examination of this alleged prophecy and its history shows a different story.

> Verily, thus saith the Lord concerning the **wars that will shortly come to pass, beginning at the rebellion of South Carolina,** which will eventually terminate in the death and misery of many souls; and the time will come that war will **be poured out upon all nations,** beginning at this place. For behold, **the Southern States shall be divided against the Northern States,** and the Southern States will call on other nations, even the nation of Great Britain, as it is called, and they shall also call upon other nations, in order to defend themselves against other nations; and then **war shall be poured out upon all nations.** And it shall come to pass, after many days, slaves shall rise up against their masters, who shall be marshaled and disciplined for war. And it shall come to pass also that **the remnants who are left of the land will marshal themselves, and shall become exceedingly angry, and shall vex the gentiles with a sore vexation.** And thus, with the sword and by bloodshed the inhabitants of the earth shall mourn; and with famine, and plague, and earthquake, and the thunder of heaven, and the fierce and vivid lightning also, shall the inhabitants of the earth be made to feel the wrath, and indignation, and chastening hand of an almighty God, until the consumption decreed **hath made a full end of all nations;** (D&C 87:1–6; December 25, 1832)

First, note the date of this revelation, December 25, 1832. The potential of a civil war was general knowledge at the time this revelation was allegedly given. The State of South Carolina passed a tariff nullification ordinance on November 24, 1832. This and northern anti-slavery agitation led to talk of armed conflict at this time. Newspapers all over the country quickly carried the unsettling news and speculation as to where events might lead. An example of how fast the news spread can be found in the *Painesville Telegraph,* dated Friday December 21, 1832, four days before Smith's alleged revelation. The *Painesville Telegraph,*

Painesville, Ohio (less than fifteen miles from Kirtland, Ohio, the new Mormon community where Joseph Smith lived), quoting from the *New York Courier and Enquirer,* reported the potential problems with South Carolina's nullification ordinance, the use of the militia, its effect on the government, and concerns for disruption and civil war. Even a Mormon newspaper, *The Evening and Morning Star* of January, 1833 (published in Independence, Missouri), featured an article titled "Rebellion in South Carolina." It described the political problems then occurring in South Carolina. So Joseph Smith's predictions were neither new nor original.

Note that Smith's prophecy says that war would be poured out on all nations. This did not happen in the Civil War or in any of the wars that followed for many decades. There also has not been "a full end of all nations" as Smith predicted.

It is interesting to note that this revelation, which is dated December 25, 1832, was not made scripture until after the Civil War. It was not published in the Book of Commandments (1833) or in the 1835 and 1844 editions of the Doctrine and Covenants. It finally appeared in the 1876 edition. (However, it was included in the first publication of the Pearl of Great Price by F. D. Richards in England in 1851.) The "revelations" proved to be only partially correct—like the frankly labeled *speculation* of other observers.

David W. Patten

On another occasion, Joseph Smith proclaimed:

Verily thus saith the Lord: it is wisdom in my servant David W. Patten, that he settle up all his business as soon as he possibly can, and make a disposition of his merchandise, **that he may perform a mission unto me next spring [spring 1839], in company with others, even twelve including himself, to testify of my name and bear glad tidings unto all the world.** (D&C 114:1, April 17, 1838)

As matters turned out David W. Patten was killed on October 25, 1838, at the age of thirty-eight at the Battle of Crooked

River, Missouri. Obviously he never went on his mission "next spring." Some Mormons would say he went on his mission in the "spirit world." But note that the alleged revelation says "next spring, in company with others, . . . [To] bear glad tidings to all the world." This must refer to an ordinary group missionary endeavor in the world we live in, not a solitary departure to the "spirit world." Smith's prediction clearly failed to prove true.

What's in a Name?

The Mormon missionaries sometimes make a point of talking about the name of the true church as mentioned in the Book of Mormon in 3 Nephi 27:6–8: ". . . therefore ye shall call the church in my name; . . . And how be it my church save it be called in my name?" They say this is the reason their church's name is the Church of Jesus Christ of Latter-day Saints.

Mormon Apostle Bruce R. McConkie said, "One or more of the names of Christ has always been used in the formal name of the church" (*Mormon Doctrine*, p. 136). Another Apostle, James E. Talmage, in speaking about 3 Nephi 27:4–12 said:

> In such wise did the Lord confirm as an authoritative bestowal, the name which, through inspiration, had been assumed by His obedient children, The Church of Jesus Christ. The Lord's explanation as to the one and only name by which the church could be appropriately known is cogent and convincing. It was not the church of Lehi or Nephi, of Mosiah or Alma, of Samuel or Helaman; else it should have been called by the name of the man whose church it was, even as today there are churches named after men; but being the church established by Jesus Christ, it could properly bear none other name[25] than His. (*Jesus the Christ*, p. 737)

From the beginning of the Mormon Church on April 6, 1830, to May 3, 1834, the name of the church was the "Church of Christ." From April 26, 1838, to the present it has been known as "The Church of Jesus Christ of Latter-day Saints" as named in the alleged revelation in Doctrine and Covenants 115:3. What was its name, however, between May 3, 1834, and April 26, 1838?

At a conference of Elders on May 3, 1834, with Joseph Smith Jr. as moderator, the name *The Church of the Latter Day Saints* was adopted by unanimous vote.[26] Does this mean that during this period, since they did not include the name of Christ, they were not Christ's? Does this mean they rejected Christ? According to 3 Nephi 27:6–8 and Apostles McConkie and Talmage that would have to be the case. Why couldn't they get their name right in the first place, if it was divinely inspired?

Proxy Work for the Dead

All the LDS ordinances—baptism, laying on of hands to receive the Holy Ghost, male ordination to the priesthood—that may be done for the living outside Mormon temples may also be executed in their temples for the deceased. There are also ordinances that can only be done in temples: endowments,[27] marriage for time and eternity, sealing of families for eternity. All of these can be done for the dead also. In temple work, a living person acts as a proxy, a stand-in, for a dead person and goes through each of the sacred ordinances. It may be a different person for each LDS ordinance. Except for baptism for the dead, in which a youth can act as a proxy, a living adult female stands in for a deceased female and a living adult male stands in for a deceased male. According to Mormon Church teachings, the deceased person then has the opportunity to accept or reject the ordinances completed in his or her behalf.

Mormon leaders consider temple work for the dead very important, as one of their top priorities. For example, they have said:

> TEMPLE WORK IS VERY IMPORTANT
> Each of us should make sure that temple work is done for ourselves and our own ancestors. The Prophet Joseph Smith taught that **the greatest responsibility we have in this world is to identify our ancestors and go to the temple in their behalf** (see *Teach-*

ings of the Prophet Joseph Smith, p. 356). Another modern prophet, Joseph Fielding Smith, said: 'Some may feel that if they pay their tithing, attend their regular meetings and duties, give of their substances to the poor . . . , spend one, two, or more years preaching the gospel in the world, that they are [free][28] from further duty. **But the greatest and grandest duty of all is to labor for the dead'** (see *Doctrines of Salvation,* 2:149). (*Gospel Principles*, pre–1988 editions, p. 248)

LDS work for the dead is viewed as a prerequisite for reaching exaltation, becoming a God. It is extremely important for a Mormon's long-term progression. The Mormon organization has put a great deal of its resources into making these teachings a reality at the local level. The world's largest genealogical library has been assembled in Salt Lake City with computer connections in major cities of the United States.

Frequently Mormons will quote 1 Corinthians 15:29 from the Bible to support their proxy temple work:

Else what shall **they** do which are baptized for the dead, if the dead rise not at all? Why are **they** then baptized for the dead? (1 Cor. 15:29)

Mormons cite this verse because Doctrine and Covenants 128:16 says:

And now, in relation to the baptism for the dead, I will give you another quotation of Paul, 1 Corinthians 15:29: Else what shall they do which are baptized for the dead, if the dead rise not at all? Why are they then baptized for the dead?

But their use of the verse is incorrect. It must be studied and understood in its context, not in isolation. The Apostle Paul in chapter 15 is speaking about the Lord's resurrection and our resurrection. In verses 1–28 and 32–58 he is addressing "we," "us," "your," and "you" (ye)—that is, fellow believers. Only in verse 29 does he say "they," evidently referring to certain persons outside the group of people he is talking to. In essence he says that even those other people, the "they," believed in the resurrection enough to baptize for the dead. Paul is not agreeing with or teaching the principle of baptism for the dead, he is just using another group of people as an example.[29]

Some Mormons may also turn for support to John 5:25 in the Bible:

> Verily, verily, I say unto you, The hour is coming, **and now is**, when the dead shall hear the voice of the Son of God: and they that hear shall live.

This verse may refer to the spiritually dead, the same dead spoken of in Ephesians 2:1, 5: "And you hath he quickened, who were dead in trespasses and sins. . . . Even when **we were dead** in sins, hath quickened us together with Christ," and in 5:14: "Wherefore he saith, Awake thou that sleepest, and arise from the dead, and Christ shall give thee light." Or it may refer to those raised from the dead by Christ in John's day. It says nothing about proxy work for the dead.

Mormons also cite these passages from 1 Peter:

> By which also he went and preached unto the spirits in prison; which sometime were disobedient, when once the longsuffering of God waited in the days of Noah, while the ark was a preparing, wherein few, that is, eight souls were saved by water. (1 Peter 3:19–20)

> For this cause was the gospel preached also to them that are dead, that they might be judged according to men in the flesh, but live according to God in the spirit. (1 Peter 4:6)

Most Christians and many Christian commentators have difficulty understanding these verses. One apologetic work offers this explanation:

> The Bible is clear that there is no second chance after death (cf. Heb. 9:27). . . . There are other ways to understand this passage, without involving a second chance at salvation after death. Some claim that it is not clear that the phrase 'spirits in prison' even refers to human beings, arguing that nowhere else is such a phrase

used of human beings in hell. They claim these spirits are fallen angels, since the 'sons of God' (fallen angels, see Job 1:6; 2:1; 38:7) were 'disobedient . . . In the days of Noah' (1 Peter 3:20; cf. Gen. 6:1–4). Peter may be referring to this in 2 Peter 2:4, where he mentions the angels sinning immediately before he refers to the Flood (v. 5).

Another interpretation is that this refers to Christ's announcement to departed spirits of the triumph of his resurrection, declaring to them the victory He had achieved by His death and resurrection, as pointed out in the previous verse (see 1 Peter 3:18). Some suggest that Jesus offered no hope of salvation to these 'spirits in prison.' They point to the fact that the text does not say Christ evangelized them, but simply that he proclaimed the victory of his resurrection to them. They insist that there is nothing stated in this passage about preaching the gospel to people in hell. . . .

1 PETER 4:6—is the gospel preached to people after they die?
PROBLEM: Peter says that 'the Gospel was preached also to those who are dead.' This appears to claim that people have a chance to be saved after they die. But this runs into conflict with Hebrews 9:27, which insists that 'it is appointed for men to die once, but after this the judgement.'

SOLUTION: in response it should be noted, first, that there is no hope held out anywhere in scripture for salvation after death. Death is final and there are only two destinies—heaven and hell, between which there is a great gulf [see Luke 16:26 about a gulf in paradise] that no one can pass over. . . . So, whatever preaching to the 'dead' may mean, it does not imply that one can be saved after he dies.

Second, this is an unclear passage, subject to many interpretations, and no doctrine should be based on an ambiguous passage like this. The difficult texts should be interpreted in the light of the clear ones and not the reverse.

Third, there are other possible interpretations of this passage that do not conflict with the teaching of the rest of scripture. (1) for example, it is possible that it refers to those who are now dead who heard the Gospel while they were alive, in favor of this is cited the fact that the Gospel 'was preached' (in the past) to those who 'are dead' (now, in the present). (2) or, some believe this might not be a reference to human beings, but to the 'spirits in prison' (angels) of 1 Peter 3:19 (cf. 2 Peter 2:4 and Gen. 6:2). (3) still others claim that, although the dead suffer the destruction of their flesh (1 Peter 4:6), yet they still live with God by virtue of what Christ did through the Gospel (namely, his death and resurrection). This victorious message was announced by Christ himself to the spirit world after his resurrection (cf. 1 Peter 3:18). (Dr. Norman Geisler and Thomas Howe, *When Critics Ask*, published by Victor Books [(SP publications, Inc.)], Wheaton, Illinois 60187, 1992, pages 533–535; quoted with permission)

The understanding of 1 Peter 3:19–20 can be helped with a reading of Luke 16:19–31:

There was a certain rich man, which was clothed in purple and fine linen, and fared sumptuously every day: and there was a certain beggar named Lazarus, which was laid at his gate, full of sores, and desiring to be fed with the crumbs which fell from the rich man's table: moreover the dogs came and licked his sores. And it came to pass, that the beggar died, and was carried by the angels into Abraham's bosom: the rich man also died, and was buried; and in hell he lift up his eyes, being in torments, and seeth Abraham afar off, and Lazarus in his bosom. And he cried and said, father Abraham, have mercy on me, and send Lazarus, that he may dip the tip of his finger in water, and cool my tongue; for I am tormented in this flame. But Abraham said, son, remember that thou in thy lifetime receivedst thy good things, and likewise Lazarus evil things: but now he is comforted, and thou art tormented. **And beside all this, between us and you there is a great gulf fixed: so that they which would pass from hence to you cannot; neither can they pass to us, that would come from thence.** Then he said, I pray thee therefore, father, that thou wouldest send him to my father's house: for I have five brethren; that he may testify unto them, lest they also come into this place of torment. Abraham saith unto him, they have Moses and the prophets; let them hear them. And he said, nay, Father Abraham: but if one went unto them from the dead, they will repent. And he said unto him, if they hear not Moses and the prophets, neither will they be persuaded, though one rose from the dead. (Luke 16:19–31)

The *great gulf fixed* prevents passage from one side to the other, leaving no allowance for proxy ordinances to get one across.

By the Spirit, Christ preached to the spirits in prison, probably like ones above. Nothing is said about the message he preached, whether there was an announcement of his resurrection or the gospel was preached as the Mormons would have us believe (there is more on this below). First Peter 4:6, which does mention the gospel being preached, is best understood in the context of the adjoining verses:

> Wherein **they** think it strange that ye run not with them to the same excess of riot, speaking evil of you. **Who** shall give account to him that is ready to judge the quick and the dead. For this cause was the gospel preached also to them that are **dead,** that **they** might be judged according to men in the flesh, but live according to God in the spirit. But the end of all things is at hand: be ye therefore sober, and watch unto prayer. (1 Peter 4:4–7)

Verse 4 speaks about the living—*they* that are in excess of riot and speaking evil. They are the living *who,* in verse 5, will have to give an account to the Lord. In verse 6 the *who* and *they* mentioned in verses 4 and 5 are the same ones that are called *dead* and the *they* that will be judged. They are all the same group, the same people. They are the same *dead* talked about in John 5:25 and Ephesians 2:1, 5; 5:14 discussed above—living people who are *dead* in sins.

First Corinthians 15:29, John 5:25, 1 Peter 3:19, and 4:6 are the only verses in the Bible that Mormons use to support baptism and proxy work for the dead. Yet these are all obscure passages, subject to varied interpretation, as noted above. In contrast, the Bible repeats many times and states quite clearly the important ordinances of the Christian church.

At this point a Mormon might say: "We have modern-day prophets to help us with confusion like this. They, with the power of God, can tell us what these verses really mean, what God really means on this subject." However, the teaching is actually refuted by LDS scripture (Bible and Book of Mormon). For example, you will not usually hear the LDS missionaries refer to the following verses from the Bible which do shed light on the subject, but which contradict LDS teaching:

> I must work the works of him that sent me, while it is day: the night cometh, when no man can work. (John 9:4)

> As I besought thee to abide still at Ephesus, when I went into Macedonia, that thou mightest charge some that they teach no other doctrine, neither give heed to fables and endless genealogies,[30] which minister questions, rather than godly edifying which is in faith: so do. (1 Tim. 1:3–4)

> But avoid foolish questions, and genealogies, and contentions, and strivings about the law; for they are unprofitable and vain. (Titus 3:9)

> None of them can by any means redeem his brother, nor give to God a ransom for him. (Ps. 49:7)

> And as it is appointed unto men once to die, but after this the judgment. (Heb. 9:27)

It is interesting to note that the Book of Mormon, the first of the unique Mormon scriptures, also has no support for baptism for the dead and in fact contradicts the teaching:

> Yea, I would that ye would come forth and harden not your hearts any longer; for behold, now is the time and the day of your salvation; and therefore, if ye will repent and harden not your hearts, immediately shall the great plan of redemption be brought about unto you. For behold, this life is the time for men to prepare to meet God; yea, behold the day of this life is the day for men to perform their labors. And now, as I said unto you before, as ye have had so many witnesses, therefore, I beseech of you that ye do not procrastinate the day of your repentance until the end; for after this day of life, which is given us to prepare for eternity, behold, if we do not improve our time while in this life, then cometh the night of darkness wherein there can be no labor performed. Ye cannot say, when ye are brought to that awful crisis, that I will repent, that I will return to my God. Nay, ye cannot say this; for that same spirit which doth possess your bodies at the time that

ye go out of this life, that same spirit will have power to possess
your body in that eternal world. For behold, if ye have procrasti-
nated the day of your repentance even until death, behold, ye have
become subjected to the spirit of the devil, and he doth seal you
his; therefore, the spirit of the Lord hath withdrawn from you, and
hath no place in you, and the devil hath all power over you; and
this is the final state of the wicked. (Alma 34:31–35)

But remember that he that persists in his own carnal nature, and
goes on in the ways of sin and rebellion against God, remaineth in
his fallen state and the devil hath all power over him. Therefore,
he is as though there was no redemption made, being an enemy to
God; and also is the devil an enemy to God. (Mosiah 16:5)

And, in fine, woe unto all those who die in their sins; for they shall
return to God, and behold his face, and remain in their sins.
(2 Nephi 9:38)

Even though the Book of Mormon is the first of the unique
LDS scriptures that the LDS missionaries will ask you to read,
they cannot use it to support baptism for the dead. This is all the
more strange, seeing that the introduction of that book says that
"the Book of Mormon . . . contains, as does the Bible, the fulness of the everlasting gospel." The fulness of the everlasting
gospel, according to Mormon leaders, is that information and
priesthood from God, which if accepted and acted upon by man
will allow him to reach exaltation.[31] But how can this be if the
Book of Mormon says work for the dead is not possible? And
how can the Bible also contain the fulness of the everlasting gospel
if it also does not support baptism for the dead (and many of the
other LDS unique teachings)?

The Doctrine and Covenants, on the other hand, contradicts
the Book of Mormon and teaches the need for Mormons to perform the sacred ordinances for their dead:

Now, the nature of this ordinance consists in the power of the
priesthood, by the revelation of Jesus Christ, wherein it is granted
that whatsoever you bind on earth shall be bound in heaven, and
whatsoever you loose on earth shall be loosed in heaven. Or, in
other words, taking a different view of the translation, whatso-

ever you record on earth shall be recorded in heaven, and whatsoever you do not record on earth shall not be recorded in heaven;
for **out of the books shall your dead be judged,** according to their
own works, whether they themselves have attended to the ordinances in their own *propria persona,* **or by the means of their own
agents,** according to the ordinance which God has prepared for
their salvation from before the foundation of the world, according to the records which they have kept concerning their dead.
. . . That which would **enable us to redeem them out of their prison;**
for the prisoners shall go free. (D&C 128:8, 22)

Including the building of the temples and the performance of ordinances therein for the **redemption of the dead,** were also in the
spirit world. (D&C 138:54)

The **dead who repent will be redeemed,** through obedience to the
ordinances of the house of God. (D&C 138:58)[32]

The question is this: which is the wisest course for the latter-day
saints to pursue—to continue to attempt to practice plural marriage, with the laws of the nation against it and the opposition of
sixty millions of people, and at the cost of the confiscation and
loss of all the temples, and the stopping of all the ordinances
therein, **both for the living and the dead,** and the imprisonment
of the First Presidency and Twelve and the heads of families in
the church, and the confiscation of personal property of the people
(all of which of themselves would stop the practice); or, after doing
and suffering what we have through our adherence to this principle to cease the practice and submit to the law, and through
doing so leave the Prophets, Apostles, and fathers at home, so
that they can instruct the people and attend to the duties of the
church, and also leave the temples in the hands of the saints, so
that they can **attend to the ordinances of the gospel, both for the
living and the dead?**
   The Lord showed me by vision and revelation exactly what
would take place if we did not stop this practice. . . . In the way
the Lord has manifested to us, and leave our Prophets and Apostles and fathers free men, and the temples in the hands of the
people, **so that the dead may be redeemed. A large number has
already been delivered from the prison house in the spirit world
by this people,** and shall the work go on or stop? (D&C Official
Declaration–1)

As the organization has done with other items, they have chosen to ignore the rejection of ordinances for the dead stated very clearly by the Book of Mormon and the Bible in order to follow the contradictory teachings of their top leaders and the Doctrine and Covenants. This needs to be brought to the attention of members of the Mormon Church. Some are not aware of it.

5

For Mormons

The Second Coming of Jesus Christ—When?

When the Lord Was Here

Ever since Jesus Christ was on the earth, people have been deeply interested in the signs of the end of the world and the time of the Lord's second coming. The Lord's disciples must have been among the earliest ones to ask:

> And as he sat upon the mount of Olives, the disciples came unto him privately, saying, Tell us, when shall these things be? and what shall be the sign of thy coming, and of the end of the world? (Matt. 24:3)

Joseph Smith's version of this verse says:

> And Jesus left them, and went upon the Mount of Olives. And as he sat upon the Mount of Olives, the disciples came unto him privately, saying: Tell us when shall these things be which thou hast said concerning the destruction of the temple, and the Jews; and what is the sign of thy coming, and of the end of the world, or the destruction of the wicked, which is the end of the world? (*Joseph Smith—Matthew,* 1:4)[1]

This question fascinated the Lord's disciples, and it has continued to interest Christians in modern times. Some, however, have gone beyond the Lord's admonition to "watch and pray" by indulging in prophetic speculation, thus assuming the role of the "false prophets" Jesus warned against (Mark 13:22, 33). Mormons may be surprised by the part their church has played.

The Millerites

Contemporary with early Mormonism, a strong second Adventist movement was started by William Miller, a Baptist living in Low Hampton, New York.[2] Miller first expressed his teachings and beliefs in 1823 and gave his first public address in August 1831 in nearby Dresden, New York.[3] He drew a following that spawned a movement that eventually spread throughout the United States. Millerites published their own newspapers, and their activity was covered by many secular papers. In January 1844 Miller stated, "I have preached about 4,500 lectures in about twelve years, to at least 500,000 people." Some estimated the Millerite movement at 30,000 to 40,000 adherents, but one observer said it peaked at about 100,000[4] in the United States. It was also estimated that the movement had as many as 1,500 lecturers spreading the message. This at a time when the early Mormon Church had worldwide membership of 17,000 in 1840 and 26,000 in 1844.[5]

The first date selected by Miller for the second coming of Jesus Christ was in the spring of 1843. When this prediction failed, March 1844, and later October 1844, became the new target dates. After the third date proved false, the movement disintegrated.[6] Diehards went on to start several Adventist denominations, the largest of which is now known as the Seventh-day Adventists.[7] Miller died December 20, 1849, but Millerite offshoots and other groups continued setting dates for the coming of the Lord.[8]

The Millerite movement was closely observed by the LDS press and members. In February 1843 Joseph Smith said, "I showed them the fallacy of Mr. Miller's data . . ." and he felt comfortable enough with the subject to give "a long exposition on Millerism."[9] *Times and Seasons*, a Mormon newspaper, had seventeen references to this subject in the February 1843 to February 1845 period. During the same two-year span, this paper made sixty-six references to the "second advent" and the "second coming." The LDS community used at least eleven terms to describe the second coming of the Lord and events associated with it. Table 2 below provides a list of these terms and the number of times they were used in various early Mormon writings.

The Mormon "Restoration" Period

Joseph Smith's interest in the Lord's second coming must have started prior to the organization of the Church. Writing several years later, he claimed to have received a visit in 1823 from the angel Moroni, who announced the imminent fulfillment of biblical prophecies:

> In addition to these, he [the angel Moroni] quoted the eleventh chapter of Isaiah, saying that it was **about to be fulfilled.** He quoted also the third chapter of Acts, twenty-second and twenty-third verses, precisely as they stand in our New Testament. He said that that prophet was Christ; but the day had not yet come when 'they who would not hear his voice should be cut off from among the people,' **but soon would come.**
>
> He also quoted the second chapter of Joel,[10] from the twenty-eighth verse to the last. He also said that this was not yet fulfilled, **but was <u>soon</u> to be.** And he further stated that the **fulness of the Gentiles**[11] **was soon to come in.** He quoted many other passages of scripture, and offered many explanations which cannot be mentioned here. . . .
>
> He commenced, and again related the very same things which he had done at his first visit,[12] without the least variation; which having done, he informed me of **great judgments which were coming upon the earth,** with great desolations by famine, sword, and pestilence; and that these grievous judgments would come on the earth **in this generation.** Having related these things, he again ascended as he had done before.[13]

Table 2 Frequency of Phrases Used in Early LDS Writings

Number of times a phrase is used in each document

Phrases used in the documents studied	E&MS	M&A	EJ	T&S	Bibl	BofM	D&C	PGP	HC	JD	TPJS	LonF	WofECM
"William Miller"*	0	0	0	0	0	0	0	0	1	0	0	0	1
"Millerism"	0	0	0	11	0	0	0	0	2	0	0	0	1
"Millerites"	0	0	0	6	0	0	0	0	0	6	0	0	3
"Second advent"	3	20	0	17	0	0	1	0	3	21	0	0	7
"Second coming"	26	13	0	49	0	0	1	0	11	78	3	0	45
"Last days"	163	153	15	332	8	5	28	4	200	700	55	4	168
"Signs of the times"	15	4	0	37	1	0	1	0	16	43	0	0	9
"Millennium"	119	14	1	53	0	0	2	0	13	96	5	0	20
"End of the world"	9	10	0	19	7	2	3	3	18	27	8	0	5
"New earth, new heaven"	2	0	0	7	1	1	2	0	2	23	0	0	0
"Latter days"	10	12	0	28	11	5	1	0	12	483	3	1	28
"New Jerusalem"	16	8	0	25	2	8	8	2	19	91	4	0	4
"Times of gentiles"	5	2	0	6	1	0	3	0	5	56	0	0	1
"Day of the Lord"	25	14	0	31	23	6	16	2	32	82	9	0	4

*See the first page of this chapter for a description of William Miller, Millerism, and Millerites.
Code: E&MS = *Evening & Morning Star* (June 1832–Sept. 1834); M&A = *Messenger & Advocate* (Oct. 1834–Sept. 1837); EJ = *Elders Journal* (Oct. 1837–Aug. 1838); T&S = *Times & Seasons* (Nov. 1839–Feb. 1846); Bibl = *Bible*, KJ Version; BofM = *Book of Mormon*; D&C = *Doctrine & Covenants*; PGP = *Pearl of Great Price*; HC = *History of the Church*; JD = *Journal of Discourses* (1855–1886); TPJS = *Teachings of the Prophet Joseph Smith*; Lonf = *Lectures on Faith*; WofECM = *Writings of Early Church Members*

Joseph Smith's alleged subsequent visits to Hill Cumorah for instruction reinforced the prophetic elements:

> Accordingly, as I had been commanded, I went at the end of each year, and at each time I found the same messenger there, and received instruction and intelligence from him at each of our interviews, respecting **what the Lord was going to do, and how and in what manner his kingdom was to be conducted** <u>in the last days.</u>[14]

After the Mormon Church's Organization

Additional alleged revelations to Joseph Smith likewise indicated that he and his followers were living in the *last days*. What follows is but a small sampling:[15]

> The rise of the Church of Christ **in these last days**, being one thousand eight hundred and thirty years since the coming of our Lord and Savior Jesus Christ, in the flesh. . . . (D&C 20:1 April 1830)

> And also with Elias, to whom I have committed the keys of bringing to pass the restoration of all things spoken by the mouth of all the holy prophets since the world began, concerning **the last days.** (D&C 27:6 Aug. 1830)

LDS Newspapers

The *signs of the times* and the *last days* were frequently discussed in the early LDS newspapers. The materials below are a small sampling from such papers:

> **SIGNS OF THE TIMES.** Signs and appearances are such, that even the most unbelieving dread coming events; and no wonder, for when the Lord comes out of his place to rebuke the nations, all hearts are faint, and all knees do tremble. (*Evening and Morning Star,* Jan. 1833, p. 62)

> No one can be mistaken, if he looks at the signs of the times as they are: **The harvest is nearly ripe. The hour of the Lord is nigh, even at the doors, and who are ready?** not the rebellious, for they

are not the blood of Ephraim. The meek only shall inherit the earth. (*Evening and Morning Star,* March 1833, p. 77)

THE GREAT DAY APPROACHES. No one can hide from the signs of the times, who has made himself acquainted with the holy scriptures. No one can hesitate, or even doubt, but that the crisis is near at hand that will try men's souls, who has searched faithfully the sacred record that was given by inspiration. **Every thing [sic] seems to whisper: The great day approaches.** (William Phelps, "Great Day Approaches," *Evening and Morning Star,* June 1833, p. 101)

Joseph Smith's Prophecy

Early in 1835 Joseph Smith gave a clear and bold statement about the Lord's second coming. The following was recorded at an official Mormon Church meeting which took place on February 14 and 15, 1835:

President Smith then stated that **the meeting had been called, because God had commanded it;** . . . and it was the will of God that those who went to Zion, with a determination to lay down their lives, if necessary, should be ordained to the ministry, and go forth to prune the vineyard for the last time, or **the coming of the Lord, which was nigh—even fifty-six years should wind up the scene** [*i.e.,* the Lord should arrive by February 16, 1891]. (*History of the Church,* 2:182)

Subsequent activity at this meeting reinforced this statement by Joseph. At this same meeting on February 14–15, 1835, twelve apostles[16] were named and nine[17] were ordained and given blessings. Heber C. Kimball, one of the nine men ordained by Oliver Cowdery, David Whitmer, and Martin Harris (three of the witnesses that allegedly saw the gold plates), relates how those ordained then had hands laid upon them by the First Presidency (Joseph Smith, Sidney Rigdon, and Frederick Williams) to confirm the blessings[18] and ordinations they had previously received.[19] Three of these blessings indicated that Christ would return during their lifetime:

The blessing of Lyman E. Johnson was, in the name of Jesus Christ, . . . and that no power of the enemy shall prevent him from going forth and doing the work of the Lord; and that **he shall live until the gathering is accomplished,** according to the holy prophets; and he shall be like unto Enoch; and his faith shall be like unto his; and he shall be called great among all the living; and Satan shall tremble before him; **and he shall see the Savior come and stand upon the earth with power and great glory.** (*History of the Church*, 2:188)

As matters turned out, Lyman E. Johnson was excommunicated from the Mormon Church on April 13, 1838, and he died in December 1856 at Prairie du Chien, Wisconsin, at age forty-five.

John F. Boynton's Blessing: . . . Thou shalt lead the elect triumphantly to the places of refuge; thou shalt be like the brethren who have been blessed before thee. **Thou shalt stand in that day of calamity when the wicked shall be consumed, and present unto the Father, spotless, the fruits of thy labor.** Thou shalt overcome all the evils that are in the world; thou shalt have wisdom to put to silence all the wisdom of the wise; and **thou shalt see the face of thy Redeemer in the flesh.** These blessings are pronounced and sealed upon thee. Even so. Amen. (*History of the Church*, 2:191)

John F. Boynton was excommunicated in 1837 and died in 1890 at the age of seventy-nine in Syracuse, New York.

William Smith's [the Prophet Joseph Smith's brother] Blessing: . . . He shall be mighty in the hands of God, in bringing about the restoration of Israel. The nations shall rejoice at the greatness of the gifts which God has bestowed upon him: that his tongue shall be loosed; he shall have power to do great things in the name of Jesus. **He shall be preserved and remain on the earth, until Christ shall come to take vengeance on the wicked.** (*History of the Church*, 2:191)

William Smith became involved with some of the off-shoots of Mormonism after his brother was killed and as a result was excommunicated October 19, 1845. He died in 1893 at the age of eighty-two at Osterdock, Iowa.

In all three cases the prophetic element of these *blessings* proved false. The Lord did not return during the lifetime of these men.

At the Church's General Conference in 1840, Joseph Smith made another clear and bold statement:

> At the April conference, 1840, the Prophet Joseph, while speaking to some of the elders on this matter said they were mistaken; the Lord would not come in ten years; no, nor in twenty years; no, nor in thirty years; no, nor in forty years, and **it will be almost fifty years before the Lord will come** [i.e., the Lord will come in about 1890].[20]

This journal entry is consistent with the *blessings* bestowed on the apostles on February 14–15, 1835. The meeting minutes of the April 1840 General Conference in the *History of the Church* and *Times and Seasons* have nothing on this subject. But another source speaks of the 1890 date:

> I. near the end of the year A.D. 1890. 45:42–44. 49:6,7. See prophecy of Joseph, uttered 14th of March, 1835. (Published in Mil.Star, NO. 13, Vol 15) 'even 56 years should wind up the scene.' Whether this had reference to the coming of Christ or to the fulfillment of the 'times of the Gentiles' is unknown.[21]

At the April 1843 General Conference, Joseph Smith continued to fuel the idea that the Lord's second coming would occur within his younger listeners' lifetime:

> Were I going to prophesy, I would say the end (of the world) would not come in 1844, 5, or 6, or in forty years. **There are those of the rising generation**[22] **who shall not taste death till Christ comes.**
>
> I was once praying earnestly upon this subject, and a voice said unto me, 'My son, if thou livest until thou art eighty-five years of age, thou shalt see the face of the Son of Man.' I was left to draw my own conclusions concerning this; and I took the liberty to conclude that if I did live to that time, He would make His appear-

ance. But I do not say whether He will make His appearance or
I shall go where He is. **I prophesy in the name of the Lord God,
and let it be written—the Son of Man will not come in the clouds
of heaven till I am eighty-five years old.** Then read the 14th chapter of Revelation, 6th and 7th verses—'And I saw another angel
fly in the midst of heaven, having the everlasting gospel to preach
unto them that dwell on the earth, and to every nation, and kindred, and tongue, and people, saying with a loud voice, Fear God
and give glory to Him, for the hour of His judgment is come.'
And Hosea, 6th chapter, After two days, etc.,—2,520 years; **which
brings it to 1890.** The coming of the Son of Man never will be—
never can be till the judgments spoken of for this hour are poured
out: **which judgments are commenced.** Paul says, 'Ye are the children of the light, and not of the darkness, that that day should
overtake you as a thief in the night.' It is not the design of the
Almighty to come upon the earth and crush it and grind it to pow-
der, but he will reveal it to His servants the prophets.[23]

An undated narrative of events similar to those in this conference report was recorded in the autobiography of Martha Thomas:

> . . . also concerning the Millerites. They were preparing a place for
> the Savior to come and meet with them, on a certain day, in that
> month in Illinois. They were making great preparations by clean-
> ing a certain piece of ground and spreading carpets, etc. Brother
> Joseph was speaking on the 'Resurrection' and the 'Second Com-
> ing of the Son of God.' 'You can go and tell Brother Miller he won't
> come on that day nor the next, nor the next year. **In the name of
> Jesus Christ I prophesy he won't come in forty years.'** . . . He was
> enquiring of the Lord concerning his second coming; the answer
> was, '**If you [Martha Thomas] live to be (I think it was eighty)
> years old you will see the face of the Son of God.'**[24]

Accepting Smith's prophetic timetable, an LDS periodical in
1845 featured a story illustrating how writers a hundred years
later (1945) would look back on apocalyptic events that would
have occurred in the 1900 time frame:

> One Hundred Years Hence, 1945, *From the Nauvoo Neighbor.*
> . . . Now the eyes of our understanding began to be quickened,

and we learned that we were one hundred years ahead of 'common life' and we glorified. . . . In digging for the foundation of our new Temple in the 124th city of Joseph, near where it is supposed the city of New York once stood. . . . It will be recollected that all the inhabitants of this city, which were spared from calamity, were 'slung out when the earth was turned upside down,' **some forty or fifty years ago [1895–1905] for their wickedness.'** (as quoted in *Millennial Star,* Oct. 15, 1845, 6:140–141)

After the Move West

After the move west, Mormon leadership was still optimistic and hopeful about the second coming of the Lord. Keeping in mind that the second coming was predicted for the 1891 time frame puts in perspective President Wilford Woodruff's remarks during the 1880s:

WE ARE LIVING AT THE COMMENCEMENT OF THE MILLENNIUM. **We are living at the commencement of the Millennium,** and near the close of the 6,000th year of the world's history. Tremendous events await this generation. . . . JD 25:10, January 6, 1884. . . .

THE SECOND COMING AT HAND. **The signs of heaven and earth all indicate the near coming of the Son of Man.** You read the 9th, 10th and 11th chapters of the last Book of Nephi, and see what the Lord has said will take place in this generation, when the gospel of Christ has again been offered to the inhabitants of the earth. **The Lord did not reveal the day of the coming of the Son of Man, but he revealed the generation. That generation is upon us.** The signs of heaven and earth predict the fulfillment of these things, and they will come to pass.—JD 21:195, July 3, 1880. . . .

WE ARE LIVING IN THE GENERATION OF CHRIST'S COMING. **We are living in the dispensation and generation to which Jesus referred**—the time appointed by God for the last six thousand years, through the mouths of all the prophets and inspired men who have lived and left their sayings on record, in which his Zion should be built up and continue upon the earth. A PROPHETIC OPINION IN 1889. Many of these young men and maidens that are here today will, in my opinion, if they are faithful, stand in the flesh when Christ comes in the clouds of heaven. These young people from the Sabbath schools and from the Mutual Improvement Associations, will stand in the flesh while the judgments of the Almighty sweep the nations of the earth as with a besom [a kind of broom, as said in a footnote][25] of destruction, in fulfillment of the revelations of God, and they will be the very people whom God will bless and sustain. Therefore, I say, our young men cannot begin too quickly to qualify themselves by treasuring up wisdom and calling upon God and getting the Holy Priesthood; for they have got to stand in holy places while these judgments are poured out upon the earth.—MS 51:595–596 (1889).[26]

These statements are a small sample of the material available.[27]

Recent History

While the LDS *standard works* still carry the message, the LDS General Authorities in recent years have not appeared to give the subject the same emphasis as in the past.

This is evidenced by articles in the Mormon magazine *Ensign*. A review of thirteen years of *Ensign* magazines 1981 through 1993 identified only two articles on the Lord's second coming. The following comment by President Ezra Taft Benson in 1986 is an example of how the subject was addressed:

Not many years hence Christ will come again. He will come in power and might as King of Kings and Lord of Lords. And ultimately "every knee shall bow and every tongue confess that Jesus is the Christ" (Rom. 14:11; D&C 88:104; Mosiah 27:31). ("Joy in Christ," *Ensign* 16 [March 1986][28]

The change in emphasis is significant as can be seen from Table 2. In a little over six years of the *Times and Seasons* (1839–1846) over 600 phrases and terms that describe the second coming were used. The *Evening and Morning Star* (1832–1834) in a little over two years had 393 usages and the *Messenger and Advocate* (1834–1837) in three years had 250 usages. Although the comparison is word/phrase usage compared to articles and references, the point is obvious. There appears to be, with only a few exceptions, a significant silence on the subject today. Why have the teachings about the second coming essentially been dropped? Could it be that the LDS leaders realize their predecessors were guilty of being false prophets, and they don't want this to be obvious to their present-day followers?[29]

The First Vision

The *First Vision* is one of the major historical and doctrinal events in the Church of Jesus Christ of Latter-day Saints. The official version may be summed up this way: On a clear spring morning in 1820, Joseph Smith, then fourteen years old, retired to woods near his home to pray. His subject: ". . . Who of all these parties [churches] are right, **or, are they all wrong together?** If any one of them be right, which is it, and how shall I know it?"[30] These questions were allegedly raised in Joseph's mind by "an unusual excitement on the subject of religion." A religious revival had allegedly occurred, and four members of Joseph's family—his mother Lucy, his brothers Hyrum and Samuel Harrison, and his sister, Sophronia, had joined the Presbyterian Church—Joseph wanted to know which church he should join.

Several notable events allegedly occurred while Joseph was in the woods praying. He was almost overcome by an evil power; his tongue was bound; a pillar of light fell upon him; he was "delivered from the enemy"; and he saw two personages, God the Father and his Son Jesus Christ. Joseph asked the personages a question: "which of all the sects was right"; and he was told all were wrong, to join none of them.

The official story was not accepted for inclusion in the *standard works* until 1880.[31] It can now be found in the Mormon scripture Pearl of Great Price.[32]

Joseph Smith's 1832 Diary Account

On pages 2 and 3 of his 1832 diary,[33] Joseph Smith wrote in his own hand an account of his First Vision and his thoughts preceding it. This is summarized in item 3 in Table 3 below. This should be compared to item 1, which is the official version now used. Both are by Joseph Smith. Several notable discrepancies are:

1. On page 2 of the diary, Joseph Smith writes: "... **by searching the scriptures** I found that mankind did **not** come unto the Lord but that they had apostatized from the true and living faith and there was no **society or denomination** that built up the gospel of Jesus Christ. . . ." On page 3 of the diary, it should be noted that Joseph does *not* ask Jesus which of the sects was right and which he should join. He already knew the answer as a result of searching the Scriptures! In the official version (JSH 1:18) Joseph *does* ask which church is true.
2. Joseph is 15 years old, not 14 as in the official version (JSH 1:7, 14).
3. No evil power is mentioned; the official version mentions an evil power (JSH 1:15–16).
4. Only one personage, Jesus, is mentioned; the official version mentions two personages, which Mormons read to be the Father and the Son (JSH 1:17–18).
5. There is no mention of the religious excitement that in the official version (JSH 1:8) provoked his need to pray.

There are over nine versions of the First Vision both from Joseph Smith and from those with whom he shared details. The table on the following pages provides a brief description of six of the main ones.

Notable Items and Differences

There are several observations worth noting about the First Vision stories. The official version did not appear in any LDS official publication until March and April 1842,[34] twenty-two years after the alleged vision. There are very significant differences between the various versions: Joseph was fourteen and fifteen years of age; an evil power was present/not present; the number of personages ranged from none to two (0–2); God the Father

Table 3 First Vision: Various Versions of Visions

Version Number When Published Brief Description	Age Year	Pillar of Light	No. of Personages	Father Present	Son Present	Question: Join What Sect?	Remarks/References
1. Official version, written 1838, first published 1842*	14 1820	yes	2	yes Both spoke	yes	Join none	Lucy, Hyrum, Samuel, Sophronia, join the Presbyterian Church. JSH, pages 49–50, 1981 Ed.; Times & Seasons, March, April 1842; Ensign, Jan. 1985, page 14; Joseph Smith's First Vision, by Milton V. Backman, Bookcraft, (Salt Lake City, 1971, 1980), Appendix C, page 160f.
2. Dictated by Smith to F. G. Williams, summer to Nov. 1832	14 or 15	yes	1	no Saw Lord, he "spoke"	yes	No question, told "None doeth good", sins forgiven	Joseph Smith's First Vision, Appendix A, page 155f.
3. Written by Smith, his 1832 diary, in his own hand	15	yes	1	no Saw the Lord Jesus Christ	yes	No question, told sins forgiven, all do no good	Ensign, Dec. 1984, pages 24–26; Ibid, Jan. 1985, page 11

Table 3 First Vision: Various Versions of Visions (continued)

Version Number When Published Brief Description	Age Year	Pillar of Light	No. of Personages	Father Present	Son Present	Question: Join What Sect?	Remarks/References
4. Smith's diary of 1835, recorded by Warren Cowdery, 11/9/1835, conversation of Smith with Joshua	about 14	yes	One then another like unto first.	? Second spoke, saw many angels.	?	No question, told sins forgiven, Jesus is Son	Joseph Smith's First Vision, Appendix B
5. Letter from Smith to John Wentworth, Ed. Chicago Democrat	none	no	2	? They spoke.	?	No question	Joseph Smith's First Vision.; Appendix D.: Ensign, Jan. 1985, page 16; Times & Seasons, Vol III, No. 9, March 1, 1842, pages 706–707.
6. Early Church leaders Brigham Young, G. A. Smith, John Taylor	15	no	1 Saw an angel, and asked the angel.	no	no	Join none	See Journal of Discourse, 2:171, 18:239; 13:77, 78; 20:167; 12:333, 334.

*There are minor differences between the various sources references, *Ensign*, Jan. 1985, p. 14.

and Jesus Christ were present/not present; angels were reported in some cases; no question was asked in some cases (join which church?); the revival that caused Joseph Smith to pray is not mentioned in all versions. The October and December 1834 and February 1835 *Messenger and Advocate* article relating the early history of the Church said nothing about the First Vision story. There is more on this below.

Note that the versions chronologically closest to the alleged actual event (items 2 and 3 in the table) differ significantly from the final official version. Also worth noting is that the version (item 6) from early members who later became high-ranking church leaders also differs significantly from the final official version.

No Revival in 1820

Using period Presbyterian and Methodist Church records and other historical sources, the Reverend Wesley P. Walters in his 26-page booklet *New Light on Mormon Origins*[35] and his book *Inventing Mormonism*[36] (with H. Michael Marquardt) clearly demonstrates that there was no revival in the Palmyra, New York, area in the 1820 period and shows that the revival actually occurred in 1824.

Evidence that there was no 1820 revival is also found in the official Mormon Church's paper of the period. In its first issue editor Oliver Cowdery[37] states that he will write a "full history" of the sect with Joseph Smith's assistance:

> . . . we have thought that a **full history** of the rise of the church of the Latter Day Saints and the most interesting parts of its progress to the present time, . . . that our narrative may be correct, and particularly the introduction, it is proper to inform our patrons, **that our brother J. Smith Jr. had offered to assist us.** (*Messenger and Advocate* 1, no. 1 [Oct. 1834]: 13)

Two months later (December 1834, p. 42)[38] he says Joseph Smith was in his fifteenth year when a religious revival resulted in his wondering which church was right. After another two months (February 1835, p. 78) he corrects what he said on page

42. He now says (apparently with Joseph Smith's assistance) that Joseph was in his seventeenth year when the religious excitement occurred. In this correction Mr. Cowdery says:

> You will recollect that I mentioned the time of a religious excitement in Palmyra and vicinity to have been in the 15th year of our brother J. Smith Jr's, age—**that was an error in the type—it should have been in the 17th**—you will please remember this correction as it will be necessary for the full understanding of what will follow in time. This would bring the date down to the year 1823. (*Messenger and Advocate* 1, no. 5 [Feb. 1835]: 78)

Oliver Cowdery continues the *full history* in the *Messenger and Advocate* on pages 78–79. He relates how on the evening of September 21, 1823, a personage sent by the commandment of the Lord visited Joseph Smith in his bedroom. Nothing is said about Joseph's praying outdoors in the *sacred Grove* and being visited by the Father and Son. The *full history* places the revival in 1823, not 1820 as in the official version (Mormon scripture, *Joseph Smith—History*, 1:1–20). It points to the conclusion that today's official version was a later invention.

In her unpublished account of the family history Lucy Mack Smith, Joseph Smith's mother, conveys similar historical information as provided by Oliver Cowdery in the *Messenger and Advocate*. She says nothing about a First Vision event in 1820 and places a "great revival in religion" that interested them after the death of her son Alvin[39] who died November 19, 1823. This must be the revival that Joseph in the present official version (*Joseph Smith—History*, 1:7) said allegedly occurred in 1820. Joseph's mother does say her son was visited by an angel[40] but nothing is said about a visitation of God the Father and Jesus Christ.

Smiths Not Living on Farm in 1820

The Reverend Wesley Walters in his article "Joseph's First Vision Story Undermined"[41] and his book *Inventing Mormonism* (with H. Michael Marquardt) uses Palmyra road tax records,[42] a Town of Manchester property tax assessment record, and other historical documents to show that the Smiths did not move from Palmyra, New York, to their farm in Manchester, New York (about two miles from the Village of Palmyra), until sometime after April 1822 and before July 1823. By using *Joseph Smith—History*, 1:5 where Joseph says that the revival occurred in the second year after their move to Manchester, Reverend Walters again shows that the revival must have occurred in 1824, not in 1820 as stated in the official version (1:3–5).

Additional evidence appears in the Smiths' genealogy, which states that Lucy Smith, the youngest child of the Smith family, was born July 18, 1821 *in Palmyra*.[43] Another indication that the Smiths were not living on their farm in Manchester, New York, in 1820 is found in *Joseph Smith—History*, 1:3, 5:

> I was born in the year of our Lord one thousand eight hundred and five, on the twenty third day of December. . . . My father . . . moved to Palmyra, Ontario (now Wayne) county, in the State of New York, when I was in my tenth year [1814–1815], or thereabouts. **In about four years [1818–1819] after my father's arrival in Palmyra, he moved with his family into Manchester in the same county of Ontario.** . . . Some time in the second year [1820–1821] **after our removal to Manchester** there was in the place where we lived an unusual excitement on the subject of religion . . . [Joseph then goes on to describe the excitement on religion and how it led to his desire to know which church to join and then his subsequent prayer and vision in the spring of 1820. (*Joseph Smith—History*, 1:14)]

According to the time calculations Joseph Smith supplies here, they moved to the farm in "Manchester" about 1818. Wayne County was not formed until April 11, 1823, and it was Ontario County prior to this, as Joseph recognized. But the area Joseph called *Manchester* did not have this name in the 1818 to 1821 time period. It was first called *Farmington*, then renamed *Burt* on March 31, 1821. It was not named *Manchester* until April 16, 1822.[44] It could be said that Joseph Smith just made a mistake in calling the town *Manchester*, but it is consistent with the other evidence to believe that Joseph Smith correctly named it

Manchester. If the revival occurred in the second year after the move to Manchester (JSH 1:5), then it occurred in 1824 (two years after April 16, 1822, at least)—a date consistent with church revival records/history and with what tax records reveal about the family's move, as shown above.

The "Explanatory Introduction" of the 1981 edition of the Doctrine and Covenants has an interesting statement on the subject of where the Smiths were living:

> During his early life he moved with his family to Manchester, in western New York. It was while **he was living <u>near</u> Manchester** in the spring of 1820, when he was fourteen years of age, that he experienced his first vision, in which he was visited in person by God, the Eternal Father, and his Son Jesus Christ.

This LDS commentary places the Smiths *near* Manchester when Joseph Smith allegedly had his First Vision.

What Did Local Newspapers Say?

In *Joseph Smith—History,* 1:21–23 and 75 Joseph Smith relates that when he shared with others the vision he had of the Father and Son, he was greatly persecuted:

> I soon found, however, that my telling the story had excited a great deal of prejudice against me among professors[45] of religion, and was the **cause of great persecution,** which continued to increase; and though I was an obscure boy, only between fourteen and fifteen years of age, and my circumstances in life such as to make a boy of no consequence in the world, yet men of high standing would take notice sufficient to **excite the public mind** against me, and **create a bitter persecution; and this was common among all the sects**—all united to persecute me. (*Joseph Smith— History,* 1:22)

> **We had been threatened with being mobbed,** from time to time, and this, too, **by professors of religion.** And their intentions of mobbing us were only counteracted by the influence of my wife's father's family (under Divine providence), who had become very

friendly to me, and who were opposed to mobs, and were willing that I should be allowed to continue the work of translation without interruption; and therefore offered and promised us protection from all unlawful proceedings, as far as in them lay. (*Joseph Smith—History*, 1:75)

It would seem that public *persecution* of the scope and magnitude described here would be noted in the local newspaper, but nothing is said. In fact, Obadiah Dogberry (a pseudonym for Abner Cole), editor of the local paper, had the following to say:

It however appears quite certain that the prophet himself never made any serious pretensions to religion until his late pretended revelation [the discovery of the Book of Mormon].[46] (*Palmyra Reflector*, February 1, 1831)

. . . It is well known that Joe Smith never pretended to any communion with angels, until a long period after the *pretended* finding of his book. . . . (*Palmyra Reflector*, article Number V, February 28, 1831)[47]

To Summarize

Four separate main lines of evidence now show that the revival was not in 1820:

1. The tax records referenced above along with *Joseph Smith—History*, 1:3–5
2. The *Messenger and Advocate* article by Oliver Cowdery
3. Presbyterian and Methodist church records
4. Joseph Smith said the town they moved to was *Manchester*

There is no evidence that there were two revivals of the magnitude described by Joseph Smith, one in 1820 and another in the 1824 time frame. The only revival that fits Joseph Smith's statement that it "became **general among all sects** in that **region of country** . . . the **whole district of country** seemed affected . . . **great multitudes** united themselves to different religious parties . . ." (*Joseph Smith—History*, 1:5) occurred in 1824. If no revival occurred in 1820, then Joseph Smith lied. If he lied, he is a false prophet, condemned by the Bible (Deut. 18:20–22; Col. 3:9; 1 Tim. 4:2). A possible explanation is that whoever wrote the current official history based it on the *Messenger and Advocate,* December 1834, page 42, and missed the correction in February 1835, page 78. This would mean the official version, a foundational event in the Mormon Church, is based upon a typographical error.

Another possible explanation of why the First Vision story changed is that Joseph Smith did not want this event to be overshadowed by vision claims of others. Visions about religion and the use of seer stones were not that unusual in the period of Joseph Smith's youth.[48] Hiram Page, an early convert who left the Mormon Church in 1838, allegedly had a vision in 1830 about the location of Zion and the New Jerusalem.[49] Early convert Solomon Chamberlain, who lived twenty miles east of Manchester when Joseph Smith was there, claimed that the Lord, through a vision, told him that all churches were corrupt and all people, with a few exceptions, were wrong.[50] Others in this same time period were reported to have had visions.[51] When the Mormons were in Kirtland, Ohio (1831–1838), the Father and Son were allegedly seen at least a dozen times at four separate sites. Joseph Smith saw many of these appearances in Kirtland.[52] He may have felt compelled to embellish his first vision account so that it would not be overshadowed by these later visions.

Pro-Mormon historian Marvin Hill, in speaking about the 1832 version (item 3 in Table 3), said:

> Merely on the face of it, the 1832 version stands a better chance of being more accurate and unembellished than the 1838 account [the official version] which was intended as a public statement, streamlined for publication. When Joseph dictated his 1838 version (if he did in fact actually dictate it), he was aware of what had been previously published by Oliver Cowdery and aware of his stature as the prophet of a new and important religious movement. **It would be natural for him to have smoothed out the story, making it more logical and compelling than perhaps it first seemed in 1820.**[53]

This pro-Mormon writer admits that Joseph Smith may have fabricated much of the first vision account.

What Some Mormons Might Say in Response

Some Mormons might point to the first four books of the New Testament to justify the conflicting versions of the First Vision. They might say, "Look at the differences between Matthew, Mark, Luke, and John. If they can have differences, then why can't Joseph Smith?" This argument ignores the fact that these gospels were penned by four different authors describing the same historical events from different perspectives, different vantage points. It is logical that one would exclude things another would include. But with the First Vision story, there is only one person telling the story. He is the one who allegedly experienced it. Yet he tells it differently each time, contradicting his own testimony. There is really no valid comparison between the gospels by Matthew, Mark, Luke, and John and the First Vision stories by one writer, Joseph Smith.

Other defenses Mormons may raise are covered in chapter 6 under "Answering Questions and Objections from Mormons."

Conclusion

Picture yourself for a moment, seated as a juror in a court of law where a criminal case is being tried. On the witness stand in his own defense, the defendant has just submitted to questioning by his attorney, during which questioning he related in detail his testimony as to what took place at the alleged crime scene. Now, as the cross-examination proceeds, the prosecuting attorney repeats the same questions. The defendant tells the story again, only this time he tells it differently. So the prosecutor asks him to go through it all a third time. When he does, he changes his story again. The clerk of the court is then asked to read aloud a statement the defendant signed shortly after his arrest, and this presents still another version of events. Summing up, the prosecutor points out that the defendant testified variously that a certain father and son were present at the scene, that only the son was present, and that neither was present; that he needed information and so asked a question, and that he already had the information and hence asked nothing; that a certain evil influence was present, and that it was not—and so on, with these and other aspects of the story changing each time it was retold. "Ladies and gentlemen of the jury," the prosecutor concludes, "I leave it to you to decide whether the defendant is a credible witness on his own behalf."

Applying the same standard of judgment leads many observers to question the LDS Church's official First Vision story. At best, it is incorrect and not supportable by historical data. At worst, the First Vision was an invention fabricated by Joseph Smith and embellished to meet changing needs in his early church. Neither possibility inspires much confidence in this foundation of Mormonism.

Perfection and Salvation

Can We Be Perfect Even as Our Father in Heaven Is Perfect?

It is appropriate to discuss the matter of becoming *perfect* and attaining *salvation*. But, first certain issues regarding the use of these words must be cleared up.[54]

Some Mormons will use Matthew 5:48 to support the LDS teaching that each man has the opportunity to reach exaltation, to become a God with all the "power, glory, dominion and knowledge" the Father and Son have.[55] Their approach is usually similar to the following: "Would God give us a commandment we could not keep? The answer is 'No' (see 1 Cor. 10:13; 1 Nephi 3:7). Let us look at a commandment in Matthew 5:48: '**Be ye therefore perfect,** even as your Father which is in heaven is perfect.'" They then go on to argue that "perfect" means to have all the attributes that make God the Father God.

Note the first word in Matthew 5:48. The Greek word *(esesthe)* that was translated here as "Be," is translated "shall be" in most usages in the Bible. A direct English translation of the

Greek manuscript would read: "shall be therefore you perfect, even as the Father your the in the heavens perfect is."[56] Mormons teach that this really means "become perfect." But there is a Greek word for "become" *(ginomai)* and it is not used in this verse in the Greek manuscript, so it is not reasonable to insert it here. If the meaning intended were "you shall be perfect," then this would turn the Lord's words into a prophetic statement, whereas "Be ye therefore perfect" is a commandment. Wording it as a commandment is consistent with the previous verses (38–47), which are commandments. In addition, the idea in "Be ye therefore perfect" is also supported by Matthew 19:21 and Hebrews 10:14, 19 (14 is shown below), which are clear. Most Christian biblical experts have consistently translated it as "Be ye therefore perfect."—Only a few render it differently: "Ye therefore shall be perfect" *The American Standard Version* (but the *New Revised Standard Version* published in 1989 has "Be perfect,"); "ye therefore shall become perfect"—*The Emphasized New Testament: A New Translation* (J. B. Rotherham); "Be then complete in righteousness"— *The New Testament in Basic English.*

From a Mormon's point of view, there should be no question on this issue. Joseph Smith in his *Joseph Smith Translation* (JST)[57] has Matthew 5:48 (numbered 5:50) as a commandment also. "Ye are therefore commanded to **be** perfect, even as your father who is in heaven is perfect." This is a far cry from *become* perfect. But you should not end the study of being perfect with this one verse. The Bible also says:

> Jesus said unto him, **If thou wilt be perfect,** go and sell that thou hast, and give to the poor, and thou shalt have treasure in heaven: and come and follow me. (Matt. 19:21)

> But let patience have her perfect work, **that ye may be perfect** and entire, wanting nothing. (James 1:4)[58]

> For by one offering he hath **perfected for ever them that are sanctified.** (Heb. 10:14[59])

From the following verses we learn that biblical prophets were perfect:

Noah was a just man and perfect in his generation, and Noah walked with God. (Gen. 6:9)

There was a man . . . whose name was **Job** and that man **was per-fect** and upright, and one that feared God, and eschewed evil. (Job 1:1)

Still we know from 1 John 1:7–10 that we are all sinners, and this includes these prophets and the other Bible authors. So the word *perfect* as used in the Bible must mean something different than being flawless,[60] *having all the attributes of God, or being a God.*

Can Mormons Be Perfect? How Does It Happen?

A verse in the Book of Mormon says:

Therefore I would that ye should **be perfect** even as I, or your Father who is in heaven is perfect. (3 Nephi 12:48)

But another part of the Book of Mormon makes a few signif-icant additions:

Yea, come unto Christ, and be perfected in him, and deny your-selves of all ungodliness;[61] and if ye shall **deny yourselves of all ungodliness and love God with all your might, mind and strength, then** is his grace sufficient for you, that by his grace ye may be perfect in Christ; and if by the grace of God ye are perfect in Christ, ye can in nowise deny the power of God. (Moroni 10:32)

This makes it a "do it yourself" activity. The phrase "**deny yourselves** of all ungodliness" means being sinless on your own! Also note the precondition of using "**all** your might, mind and strength" in loving God. Once these are done, then and only then does the God of Mormonism grant his grace. Can a Mormon become sinless before this happens? If he could, why would he have further need of the grace of God?

The Mormon needs to be shown that there is nothing we can do to save[62] ourselves; that is, to spend eternity with God when we die. We cannot make it under the Mosaic law by trying to obey God's commandments under our own strength, for it is clear in the Bible that we are all sinners. It is not possible for us, under our own power, to be good enough. There is only one way: accept Jesus Christ as your Lord and Savior and accept his free grace. When this happens, we are justified and sanctified in the sight of the Father. The blood and death of our Savior cleanses us of our sins, and we are perfect in the eyes of God. What follows shows how this happens now, while we are alive on earth, and how it continues.

Trying to Keep the Law Will Not Save Us

The Bible is clear that only a relatively *few* will receive eternal life; that is, spend eternity with God:

> Enter ye in at the strait gate: for wide is the gate, and broad is the way, that leadeth to destruction, and many there be which go in thereat: Because strait is the gate, and narrow is the way, which leadeth unto life, and **few there be that find it.** (Matt. 7:13–14)

It is also clear that we will not do it by trying to keep the law.

> For whosoever shall keep the whole law, and yet **offend in one point, he is guilty of all.** (James 2:10)[63]

> For as many as are of the works of the law are under the curse: for it is written, **Cursed is every one that continueth not in all things** which are written in the book of the law to do them. (Gal. 3:10)

We Cannot Do It Ourselves Because We Are All Sinners!

It also will not happen because we are all sinners.

> As it is written, **There is none righteous, no, not one.** . . . For **all have sinned,** and come short of the glory of God. (Rom. 3:10, 23)

If we say that we have no sin, we deceive ourselves, and the truth is not in us . . . If we say that we have not sinned, we make him a liar, and his word is not in us. (1 John 1:8, 10)

But There Is a Way!

But there is a way! Jesus Christ is the way, the truth, and the life (John 14:6) and he is the door to salvation (John 10:9):

For **Christ is the end of the law** for righteousness to every one that believeth. (Rom. 10:4)

But if we walk in the light, as he is in the light, we have fellowship one with another, and the **blood of Jesus Christ his Son cleanseth us from all sin . . . If we confess**[64] **our sins,** he is faithful and just to forgive us our sins, and to cleanse us from all unrighteousness. (1 John 1:7, 9)

This is a faithful saying, and worthy of all acceptation, that **Christ Jesus came into the world to save sinners;** of whom I am chief. (1 Tim. 1:15)

Unfortunately there is a hidden clause in the contract Mormons have with their God. For a Mormon, holding onto his salvation is going to be a very tough job. He had better not stumble too many times, for it appears that the Mormon God has a limited supply of mercy and grace. Mormon scripture says:

And now, verily I say unto you, I, the Lord, will not lay any sin to your charge; go your ways **and sin no more;** but unto that soul who sinneth [again] shall the **former sins return,** saith the Lord your God. (D&C 82:7)

A Mormon prophet (Spencer W. Kimball) explains:

We can hardly be too forceful in reminding people that they cannot sin and be forgiven and then sin again and again and expect repeated forgiveness.[65]

We know of nothing in the Bible (or even the Book of Mormon) that says the faithful and honest confessed and repentant sinner will eventually be ignored by God. In fact, the Bible says God will *not* remember our sins:

> And they shall teach no more every man his neighbour, and every man his brother, saying, Know the LORD: for they shall all know me, from the least of them unto the greatest of them, saith the LORD: for I will forgive their iniquity, and **I will remember their sin no more.** (Jer. 31:34)

> I, even I, am he that blotteth out thy transgressions for mine own sake, and **will not remember thy sins.** (Isa. 43:25)

> As far as the east is from the west, so far hath he removed our transgressions from us. (Ps. 103:12)

Only by the Grace of God, through Faith, Are We Forgiven and Saved!

To Mormons grace[66] is one of the most difficult ideas to understand. They believe they have to work their way to spend eternity with God:

> Even when we were dead in sins, hath quickened us together with Christ, **(by grace ye are saved).** . . . **For by grace are ye saved through faith;** and that not of yourselves: it is the gift of God. (Eph. 2:5, 8)[67]

> But we believe that **through the grace of the Lord Jesus Christ we shall be saved,** even as they. (Acts 15:11)

> Who hath saved us, and called us with an holy calling, **not according to our works,** but according to **his own purpose and grace,** which was given us in Christ Jesus before the world began. (2 Tim. 1:9)

However, the Book of Mormon nullifies this concept:

> . . . for we know that it is by grace we are saved, **after all we can do.** (2 Nephi 25:23)

And he commandeth all men that they must repent, and be baptized in his name, **having perfect faith** in the Holy One of Israel, or they cannot be saved in the kingdom of God. (2 Nephi 9:23)

Yea, come unto Christ, and be perfected in him, and deny yourselves of all ungodliness; and if ye shall **deny yourselves of all ungodliness,** and love God with **all your might, mind and strength,** then is **his grace sufficient** for you, that by his grace ye may be perfect in Christ; and if by the grace of God ye are perfect in Christ, ye can in nowise deny the power of God. (Moroni 10:32)

Can any of us always do all we can? Do we always have perfect faith? Can we deny ourselves of all ungodliness and love God with all our mind, might, and strength day after day, year after year, and decade after decade without a slip-up? Yet this is what Mormonism requires before God's grace is given.

Do We Only Have to Just Say the Words "We Believe"?

Not understanding grace, Mormons will be incredulous, and maybe even ridicule the idea. They might say, "You mean all you have to do is say the right words, and then it is okay to live a life of sin?" The Apostle Paul experienced the same question. He answered it in his Epistle to the Romans:

For sin shall not have dominion over you: for ye are not under the law, but under grace. **What then? shall we sin, because we are not under the law, but under grace? God forbid.** Know ye not, that to whom ye yield yourselves servants to obey, his servants ye are to whom ye obey; whether of sin unto death, or of obedience unto righteousness? But God be thanked, that ye **were the servants of sin, but ye have obeyed from the heart that form of doctrine which was delivered you.** Being then made free from sin, ye became the servants of righteousness. (Rom. 6:14–18)

The Apostle expands on this further on:

That if thou shalt **confess with thy mouth** the Lord Jesus, and shalt **believe in thine heart** that God hath raised him from the dead, **thou shalt be saved. For with the heart man believeth unto righteousness;** and with the mouth confession is made unto salvation. (Rom. 10:9–10)

Paul makes it clear that not only must each of us tell people that Christ is our Lord and Savior; we must also believe it in our hearts. The belief in our hearts will then lead us to live the Savior's commandments, to want to please him.

We Can Know Now That We Are Saved and Have Eternal Life!

Many Mormons do not feel they can know where they will spend eternity, so it is possible that you will get disagreement here also. In reading the verses below, note carefully that the tenses of the verbs are *in the present*. We can know *now* where we will spend eternity.

For God so loved the world, that he gave his only begotten Son, that whosoever believeth in him should not perish, **but have everlasting life. . . . He that believeth on the Son**[68] **hath everlasting life:** and he that believeth not the Son shall not see life; but the wrath of God abideth on him. (John 3:16, 36)

Verily, verily, I say unto you, He that heareth my word, and **believeth on him that sent me, hath everlasting life,** and shall not come into condemnation; but is passed from death unto life. (John 5:24)

Verily, verily, I say unto you, He that believeth on me hath everlasting life. . . . Whoso eateth my flesh, and drinketh my blood, **hath eternal life;** and I will raise him up at the last day. (John 6:47, 54)

These things have I written unto you **that believe on the name of the Son of God; that ye may know that ye have eternal life,** and that ye may believe on the name of the Son of God. (1 John 5:13)[69]

First Corinthians 1:18, 2 Timothy 1:9, Romans 8:24, and 1 Corinthians 15:2 say the same thing.

We Can Be Perfect Even as Our Father in Heaven Is Perfect—Now!

This idea will be incomprehensible to most Mormons (and some Christians). All their Mormon life they have been taught that they can *become* a God, but not in this life. It will take an eternity and will occur after they are resurrected. Matthew 5:48 is the most quoted reference. A Mormon prophet (Spencer W. Kimball) said:

> **We are gods in embryo,** and the Lord demands perfection of us.[70]

A training manual published by the Mormon Church says:

> MEN ARE GODS IN EMBRYO
> We Have the Potential to Become like Our Heavenly Parents
> 'Man is the child of God, formed in the divine image . . . is capable, by experience through ages of aeons, of evolving into a God.' (The First Presidency [Joseph F. Smith, John R. Winder, Anthon H. Lund], 'The Origin of Man,' *Improvement Era,* Nov. 1909, p. 81)[71]

There is a long list of items a Mormon *must obey in this life* before this can happen. One such list says:

> Latter-day Saints are taught that **now is the time to fulfill the requirements for exaltation**[72] (see Alma 34:32–34). President Joseph Fielding Smith said, "In order to obtain the [sic] exaltation we must accept the gospel[73] and all its covenants; and take upon us the obligations which the Lord has offered; and walk in the light and understanding of the truth; and **'live by every word** that proceedeth forth from the mouth of God'" (Doctrines of Salvation, 2:43).

There are specific ordinances we must have received to be exalted:

1. We must be baptized and confirmed a member of the Church of Jesus Christ.[74]
2. We must receive the Holy Ghost.
3. We must receive the temple endowments.
4. We must be married for time and all eternity.

In addition to the required ordinances, there are also many laws we have to obey to qualify for exaltation. We must—

1. Love God and worship him.
2. Have faith in Jesus Christ.
3. Live the law of chastity.
4. Repent of our wrong doings.
5. Pay honest tithes and offerings.
6. Be honest in our dealings with others and with the Lord.
7. Speak the truth always.
8. Obey the Word of Wisdom.[75]
9. Search out our kindred dead and perform the saving ordinances of the gospel for them.[76]
10. Keep the Sabbath day holy.
11. Attend our Church meetings as regularly as possible to renew our baptismal covenants. This is done as we partake of the sacrament.
12. Love and strengthen our family members in the ways of the Lord.
13. Have family and individual prayers every day.
14. Honor our parents.
15. Teach the gospel to others by word and example.
16. Study the scriptures.
17. Listen to and obey the words of the prophets of the Lord.
18. Develop true charity in our lives.

In other words, each person must endure in faithfulness, **keeping all the Lord's commandments** until the end of his life on earth. (*Gospel Principles*, pp. 291–92)

Notice that it says "keeping all the Lord's commandments" in this life. Item 17, "obey the words of the prophets," actually expands into another long list of items that must be obeyed.

A Mormon who is honest will have to admit that he or she can achieve, at best, only partial compliance with these requirements. Christians, too, experience many failures in areas they share as goals—speaking the truth, praying regularly, regular Scripture study, doing good for others, honoring our parents, and so on— but happily, we do not depend on these works for our standing with God.

We Are Justified by Jesus Christ

Mormon Apostle Bruce R. McConkie makes it clear that the burden is all on the Mormon:

What then is the law of justification? . . . As with all other doctrines of salvation, justification is available because of the atoning sacrifice of Christ, but it becomes operative in the life of an individual **only on conditions of personal righteousness.** (*Mormon Doctrine,* p. 408, under "Justification")

Fortunately the Bible has a different message! We are justified by the death and blood of Jesus Christ. In other words, we are found "not guilty," we are acquitted, declared righteous, and made sinless and holy before God. The Bible says:

And **by him all that believe are justified from all things,** from which ye could not be justified by the law of Moses. (Acts 13:39)

Being justified freely by his grace through the redemption that is in Christ Jesus. . . . Therefore we conclude that a **man is justified by faith** without the deeds of the law. (Rom. 3:24, 28)

That being **justified by his grace,** we should be made heirs according to the hope of eternal life. (Titus 3:7)

A Mormon scripture also has a similar message, but for some reason it is ignored:

For by the water ye keep the commandment; by **the Spirit ye are justified,** and **by the blood ye are sanctified;** (Moses 6:60)

Romans 5:1, 9; 8:30; 1 Corinthians 6:11; Galatians 2:16, 17; 3:11, 24 also say the same thing.

We Are Sanctified by Jesus Christ

Mormon Apostle Bruce R. McConkie continues to place the burden on Mormons:

To be sanctified is to become clean, pure, and spotless; to be free from the blood and sins of the world; to become a new creature of the Holy Ghost, one whose body has been renewed by the rebirth of the Spirit. Sanctification is **a state of saintliness, a state attained only by conformity to the laws and ordinances of the gospel.** The plan of salvation is the system and means provided **whereby men may sanctify their souls and thereby become worthy** of a celestial inheritance. . . . Those who are faithful in magnifying their callings in the Melchizedek Priesthood "are sanctified by the Spirit unto the renewing of their bodies." (D&C 84:33) . . . **Sanctification is a personal reward that follows personal righteousness.** (*Mormon Doctrine*, pp. 675–676, under "Sanctification")

The biblical message again is different. Sanctification "concerns the moral and spiritual transformation of the justified believer who is regenerated, given new life by God."[77] The Bible teaches that perfection now, in this life, is possible through the sanctification of our Lord Jesus Christ:

Unto the church of God which is at Corinth, to them that **are sanctified in Christ Jesus,** called to be saints, with all that in every place call upon the name of Jesus Christ our Lord, both theirs and ours. (1 Cor. 1:2)

And such were some of you: but ye are washed, **but ye are sanctified,** but ye **are justified** [acquitted] in the name of the Lord Jesus, and by the Spirit of our God. (1 Cor. 6:11)

For by one offering **he hath perfected for ever them that are sanctified.** (Heb. 10:14)

Jude, the servant of Jesus Christ, and brother of James, to them **that are sanctified by God the Father, and preserved in Jesus Christ, and called.** (Jude 1:1)

And now, brethren, I commend you to God, and to the word of his grace, which is able to build you up, and to give you an inheritance **among all them which are sanctified.** (Acts 20:32)

To open their eyes, and to turn them from darkness to light, and from the power of Satan unto God, that they may receive forgiveness of sins, and inheritance among them which **are sanctified by faith that is in me.** (Acts 26:18)

Only one conclusion is possible. The Bible is telling us we can be *perfect* in this life, in the eyes of God, because of our faith in Jesus Christ and his grace. We are sinners, but because of the blood of Jesus Christ—through our confession, repentance, and faith in him—our sins are not seen by the Father. Our sins are cleansed (1 John 1:7, 9) by the blood of Jesus Christ; therefore we are perfect *now* in the sight of God!

Mormons need to recognize that it is impossible for them to obey all the laws of Mormonism in this life. LDS teaching, as shown above, makes it clear that they had better not stumble too often, otherwise they will be carrying all their sins—past, present, and new ones—all at once, all alone.

In your discussions, stress the impossibility of doing everything Mormonism requires. If they say the grace of God will help them, remind them of 2 Nephi 25:23 *(saved by grace after all we can do)*, 2 Nephi 9:23 *(having perfect faith)*, and Moroni 10:32 *(deny yourself of all ungodliness)*. Walk them through the list of what they need to do. Have them explain in detail how they are doing *for each item*. Ask them if they have ever stumbled, and then remind them of Doctrine and Covenants 82:7 *(new sin causes the weight of forgiven sins of the past to return)* and of what President Spencer Kimball said *(we cannot expect repeated forgiveness)*. Ask them if they might not stumble again and again. Ask if there is any hope for them. Then by reading many of the Bible references above show what Jesus Christ can do for them.

People of African Heritage and the Mormon Church

Prior to September 1978, anyone of African racial ancestry could not hold any of the Mormon priesthoods. On September 30, 1978, the first presidency of the Mormon Church presented what is now Official Declaration—2 in the Doctrine and Covenants. It allowed all men to qualify for the Mormon priesthood, with all the rights and authority of that priesthood, without regard for race or color.

Over 150 years of Mormon Priesthood discrimination against men of African heritage came to an end. Even with this revelation, however, black people may not want to accept this at face value. They may want to examine the history of their people in the Mormon Church. How have black people been treated, and what have Mormon prophets said about them? It must be noted that when the Mormon Church began in 1830, many white Christian churches held the view that black people were descended from Cain and therefore cursed to be slaves. Segregation was the rule. Christians ignored Paul's teaching that "there is neither Jew nor Greek, there is neither bond nor free, there is neither male nor female: for ye are all one in Christ Jesus" (Gal. 3:28).

Early in its history, after a short period of indecision, the Mormon Church instituted a practice of priesthood segregation. Black men could not hold the Mormon priesthood, had no authority to act in God's name, and had no priesthood status; therefore, they could not take part in temple rituals and eventually become Gods. But was there more than this? It must be noted that early Mormon Prophets and Presidents Joseph Smith, Brigham Young, John Taylor, and other top leaders who followed them, claimed to be more than clergymen. They claimed to be prophets of God. They led the "one true church." They were the only ones with authority to speak for God.[78] Why did they ignore Galatians 3:28 or even their own special canonized scripture, the Book of Mormon? In 2 Nephi 26:33 we find: ". . . he inviteth them all to come unto him . . . denieth none that come . . . black and white, bond and free, male and female. . . ." Perhaps they were more influenced by other Book of Mormon references—1 Nephi 12:23, 2 Nephi 5:21, Jacob 3:5, Alma 3:6–9 Mormon 5:15, and in the 1830 edition, chapter 12, page 117—which portray a white or light skin as a sign of righteousness and a black or dark skin as a sign of unrighteousness. These scriptures are still used by the Mormon Church. Nephi 30:6 originally stated that one's skin color would change to "white and delightsome" when one knows correct teachings. Subsequent to the alleged revelation in 1978 giving the priesthood to African-American men, this phrase was changed to "pure and delightsome."

The following quotes from top Mormon leaders and official LDS publications are given to demonstrate the Mormon Church's position about black people in the past:

> . . . Cain conversed with his God every day, and knew all about the plan of creating this earth, for his father told him. But, for the want of humility, and through jealousy, and an anxiety to possess the kingdom, and to have the whole of it under his own control and not allow any body else the right to say one word, what did he do? He killed his brother. The Lord put a mark on him; and there are some of his children in this room. When all the other children of Adam have had the privilege of receiving the Priesthood, and of coming into the kingdom of God, and of being redeemed from the four quarters of the earth, and have received their resurrection from the dead, then it will be time enough to remove the curse from Cain and his posterity. . . . he is the last to share the joys of the kingdom of God. . . . (Brigham Young, Dec. 12, 1854, *Journal of Discourses*, 2:142–143)

> You see some classes of the human family that are black, uncouth, uncomely, disagreeable and low in their habits, wild, and seemingly deprived of nearly all the blessings of the intelligence that is generally bestowed upon mankind. . . . How long is that race to endure the dreadful curse that is upon them? That curse will remain upon them, and they never can hold the Priesthood or share in it until all the other descendants of Adam have received the promises and enjoyed the blessings of the Priesthood and the keys thereof. Until the last ones of the residue of Adam's children are brought up to that favourable position, the children of Cain cannot receive the first ordinances of the Priesthood. They were the first that were cursed, and they will be the last from whom the curse will be removed. When the residue of the family of Adam come up and receive their blessings, then the curse will be removed from the seed of Cain, and they will receive blessings in like proportion. (Brigham Young, Oct. 9, 1859, *Journal of Discourses*, 7:290–291)

Shall I tell you the law of God in regard to the African race? If the white man who belongs to the chosen seed mixes his blood with the seed of Cain, the penalty, under the law of God, is death on the spot. *This will always be so.* (Brigham Young, March 8, 1863, *Journal of Discourses*, 10:110)

Brigham Young's successor, John Taylor, declared:

. . . after the flood we are told that the curse that had been pronounced upon Cain was continued through Ham's wife, as he had married a wife of that seed. And why did it pass through the flood? **Because it was necessary that the devil should have a representation upon the earth.** . . . (John Taylor, Aug. 28, 1881, *Journal of Discourses*, 22:304)

In past Mormon theology, a black skin is a sign of God's displeasure. In the Mormon Sunday school publication, *Juvenile Instructor,* the following statement appeared:

We will first inquire into the results of the approbation or displeasure of God upon a people, starting with the belief that a **black skin is a mark of the curse of Heaven placed upon some portions of mankind.** Some, however, will argue that a black skin is not a curse, nor a white skin a blessing. In fact, some have been so foolish as to believe and say that a black skin is a blessing, and that the negro is the finest type of a perfect man that exists on the earth; but to us such teachings are foolishness. **We understand that when God made man in his own image and pronounced him very good, that he made him white.** We have no record of any of God's favored servants being of a black race . . . every angel who ever brought a message of God's mercy to man was beautiful to look upon, clad in the purest white and with a countenance bright as the noonday sun. ([Oct. 15, 1868] 3:157).

Another LDS apostle said the following:

There is a reason why one man is born black and with other disadvantages, while another is born white with great advantages. The reason is that we once had an estate before we came here, and were obedient, more or less, to the laws that were given us there. Those who were faithful in all things there received greater blessings here, and those who were not faithful received less. . . . There were no neutrals in the war in heaven. All took sides either with Christ or with Satan. Every man had his agency there, and men receive rewards here based upon their actions there, just as they will receive rewards hereafter for deeds done in the body. The Negro, evidently, is receiving the reward he merits. (Joseph Fielding Smith, *Doctrines of Salvation,* 1954, 1:61, 65–66)

John J. Stewart, in his book *Mormonism and the Negro,* quotes from a letter from the First Presidency of the Mormon Church dated July 17, 1947: "From the days of the Prophet Joseph even until now, it has been the doctrine of the Church, never questioned by the church leaders, that the Negroes are not entitled to the full blessings of the gospel" (pp. 46–47).

The late Mormon Apostle Bruce R. McConkie, in an early edition of his popular compendium of Mormon teachings, *Mormon Doctrine,* says:

. . . Those who were less valiant in pre-existence and who thereby had certain spiritual restrictions imposed upon them during mortality are known to us as the negroes. Such spirits are sent to earth through the lineage of Cain, the mark put upon him for his rebellion against God and his murder of Abel being a black skin. (Moses 5:16–41; 7:8, 12, 22.) Noah's son Ham married Egyptus, a descendant of Cain, thus preserving the negro lineage through the flood. (Abra. 1:20–27.) Negroes in this life are denied the priesthood; under no circumstances can they hold this delegation of authority from the Almighty.[79]

Do these statements sound like something one would expect from God's "one true church"? Since President Kimball's 1978 revelation, the only thing that changed was that black men could now hold the priesthood. Nothing has been said that changes the unique Mormon teaching on the pre-existence. The teaching that the conduct of spirits in the pre-existence (the pre-mortal state) affects the conditions and circumstances of their mortality,[80] is still in place.

In addition, nothing has been said that changes the Book of Mormon verses that say that a white skin is a sign of righteousness and a black or dark skin is a sign of unrighteousness. Nor have Mormon scriptures Moses 7:8, 22, where blackness came on the children of Canaan, and they were despised, been changed. Although the Mormon Church does not talk about them anymore, these teachings are all still in place. According to the Mormon scriptures, white is righteous, clean, pure; black or dark is unrighteous, dirty, impure.

There is no biblical support for these non-Christian teachings on pre-existence and skin color! In fact, the Bible teaches otherwise. Contradicting the Mormon teaching of pre-existence, the Bible says:

And the LORD God formed man of the dust . . . and breathed into his nostrils the breath of life. (Gen. 2:7)

Howbeit that was not first which is spiritual, but that which is natural; and afterward that which is spiritual. (1 Cor. 15:46)[81]

. . . the LORD, which stretcheth forth the heavens . . . and formeth the spirit of man within him.[82] (Zech. 12:1)

In Job 38:1–4, 18, 21, Job is asked where he was when the earth was formed; and in 40:3–5, 42:1–3 he doesn't know the answer. Why? Because he didn't exist! In John 3:6 we read: "That which is born of the flesh is flesh." Therefore, a God with a body of flesh and bones, as the Mormon God has, could not procreate "spirit" children!

The Bible teaches that all believers are equal before God:

For as many as are led by the Spirit of God, they are the Sons of God. (Rom. 8:14)

For ye are all the children of God by faith in Christ Jesus. (Gal. 3:26)

and [God] hath made of one blood all nations of men. . . . (Acts 17:26)

There is neither Jew nor Greek, there is neither bond nor free, there is neither male nor female: for ye are all one in Christ Jesus. (Gal. 3:28)

Although not excusable, it is understandable how self-interest and sinfulness could lead whole churches and denominations to ignore these biblical principles. But would God's "one true church," led by real true prophets of God for over 150 years ignore God's Word and teach such non-Christian/non-biblical doctrine? And would God wait until the Civil Rights movement finished its work before inspiring Official Declaration—2?

We should note that although the past teachings of the top Mormon leaders and two of the canonized scriptures of the Mormon Church are clearly discriminatory against men of African heritage, it is our opinion that most members of the Mormon Church are not. Many are either not even aware of the historical information or have not considered in total the many LDS scriptures referenced.[83]

6

Responses–Mormons' and Yours

Sooner or later when you witness to Mormons, you will hear something like: "We don't attack you. Why are you attacking us? Why do you speak against our Church? We should only say good things about each other!" This is usually said with sincerity and a hurt look. Is this argument correct? No, it is not! The Mormon Church does attack Christians and other churches. In fact, it was the Mormon Church that initiated the battle and forced Christians to take up defensive positions. Mormon leaders have attacked Christianity since 1830, and their attacks continue to the present in canonized LDS scriptures still in use. Only in recent decades has the LDS Church stopped attacking Christianity in its newer publications. Examples from LDS scriptures still in use today begin with Joseph Smith's First Vision story:

> My object in going to inquire of the Lord was to know which of all the sects was right, that I might know which to join. No sooner, therefore, did I get possession of myself, so as to be able to speak, than I asked the Personages who stood above me in the light, **which of all the sects was right** (for at this time it had never entered into my heart that all were wrong)—and **which I should join.** I

was answered that I must **join none of them, for they were all wrong;** and the Personage who addressed me said that all **their creeds were an abomination in his sight; that those professors were all corrupt;** that: "they draw near to me with their lips, but their hearts are far from me, they teach for doctrines the commandments of men, having a form of godliness, but they deny the power thereof. . . . And as I leaned up to the fireplace, mother inquired what the matter was. I replied, 'Never mind, all is well— I am well enough off.' I then said to my mother, '**I have learned for myself that Presbyterianism is not true.**' (*Joseph Smith—History,* 1:18–20)[1]

Some Mormons are ashamed of this attack and try to minimize it. They try to say it only applied to the churches in 1820. However, there is no official Mormon Church publication that says anything to this effect.[2] The content of the quote clearly shows it would be applicable now. Earlier, in *Joseph Smith— History,* 1:5–9, we learned that the *sects* mentioned in 1:18 are the Baptists, Methodists, and Presbyterians. The beliefs and creeds of these churches are essentially the same now as they were in 1820; so if they were an abomination to God in 1820, they would still be now. The *professors* are not teachers, as some would have us believe,[3] but everyone who accepted the creeds and gave a public profession of their acceptance.[4] If those professing these creeds were corrupt in 1820, they must be now also. Note in verse 20 the clear statement by Joseph Smith that he had learned "that Presbyterianism is not true." Christians naturally take the position that we do not believe God spoke these things to Joseph Smith, and that we are offended by them and want to defend ourselves.

The next quote from the Book of Mormon is of a similar nature:

And he said unto me: Behold there **are save two churches only; the one is the church of the Lamb of God, and the other is the church of the devil;** wherefore, whoso belongeth not to the church of the Lamb of God belongeth to that great church, which is the mother of abominations; and she is the whore of all the earth. (1 Nephi 14:10)

In speaking to Mormons about this verse, we should point out that the Mormon Church claims to be the church of the Lamb of God (see appendix 1)—consigning the rest of us to the church of the devil. Some Mormons will not admit this, so we may need to quote the following statements, allegedly by Jesus Christ, as recorded in the Doctrine and Covenants:

> And also those to whom these commandments were given, might have power to lay the foundation of this church, and to bring it forth out of obscurity and out of darkness, **the only true and living church upon the face of the whole earth,** with which I, the Lord, am well pleased, speaking unto the church collectively and not individually. (D&C 1:29–30)

Mormon Apostle Bruce R. McConkie, as quoted in a Mormon Church teaching manual, defined the church of the devil as follows:

> . . . **It is every church except the true church,** whether parading under a Christian or a pagan banner. . . .[5]

The following excerpt is from a Mormon Church booklet:

> The Lord provided that salvation should come through his gospel, functioning through his church, . . . But where is there such a church? . . . Is there such a church upon the earth? . . . **Until 1830 there was not** . . . In 1830 the Almighty restored his church to earth again. . . . This restored church is known as The Church of Jesus Christ of Latter-day Saints, with headquarters in Salt Lake City.[6]

Once we have established that "the church of the Lamb of God" referenced in 1 Nephi 14:10 is the Mormon Church we then ask: What is the "church of the devil"? The answer is obvious, but frequently Mormons will try not to verbalize it. So we need to. We need to tell them we are offended by this verse implying our church is included in the "church of the devil." The above statements are spread all over the world by the hundreds of thousands in the Pearl of Great Price (which contains *Joseph Smith—History,* 1:18–20 and is usually bound with the D&C) and by the millions in the Book of Mormon (which contains 1 Nephi 14:10). Surely we should be allowed to defend ourselves.

In addition to their unique scriptures, top LDS leaders have also attacked Christianity in their other books, articles, and speeches. Two examples, one old one and a newer one are:

> . . . **I said their baptisms are illegal.** . . . Says one—'you mean to say that all our marriages are also illegal, as well as our baptisms?' Yes I do, as far as God is concerned . . . **in the sight of heaven these marriages are illegal, and the children illegitimate.** (Apostle Orson Pratt, August 31, 1873, *Journal of Discourses*, 16:175–176)

> The false gods of Christendom bear the same names as the true Gods of the Bible. Beyond this they have little resemblance. They are described in the creeds that the Lord told Joseph Smith were 'an abomination in his sight.' (JS-H 1:19). (Apostle Bruce R. McConkie, *A New Witness for the Articles of Faith*, p. 55)[7]

In the past fifteen years or so, the Mormon Church's publications have taken a more positive approach. Expending large sums of money on TV advertising and a far-reaching public relations program to improve the image of the LDS Church, Mormon leaders no longer attack other churches openly as they once did.

Mormons need to understand that we witness to them because we are commanded to do so (see the beginning of chapter 1) and also to defend our faith from attacks initiated by Mormonism.

It Doesn't Mean That . . .

Many Mormons, in an effort to rationalize the material quoted in this book, may try to change the meaning of some of the words or phrases in the statements. They may also try to add words, all in an effort to have the reference harmonize with what the Mormon Church or its other scriptures say. Let us look at what Joseph Smith and the Book of Mormon say about this:

Now taking it for granted that the scriptures **say what they mean, and mean what they say,** we have sufficient grounds to go on. . . . (*Teachings of The Prophet Joseph Smith*, p. 264; *Times and Seasons*, Sept. 1, 1842, 3:904)

. . . Behold, the scriptures are before you; **if ye will wrest them it shall be to your own destruction.** (Alma 13:20)

It seems reasonable to assume that Scriptures are worded correctly. We should not force words and phrases into a meaning not there. The same logic should be applicable to the words of LDS prophets and top leaders. Those who refuse to use this application should consider the following questions: What is my authority to change the meaning of words by Joseph Smith (or whatever the source is)? Was he incapable of saying what he meant? I know Joseph Smith's authority (founding prophet and first president) in the Mormon Church—what is mine that I can change what a prophet says? Is there an official LDS Church statement agreeing with what I am saying? If there is none, I must realize I am just giving my personal opinion. It is interesting, but not authoritative!

Some may try to claim an authority they do not have. They must not understand the *very high* authority top LDS leaders claim when the subject is Church doctrine and teachings. It exceeds the authority of anyone else, including LDS Church members. The following is a small sample of quotes showing this (there are more in appendix 4):

At the conclusion of one general conference, President Kimball [the president and prophet] said: "Now as we conclude this general conference, let us all give heed to what was said to us. Let us assume the counsel given applies to *us*, to me. Let us **hearken to those we sustain as prophets and seers, as well as the other brethren** [general authorities/top leaders], as if our eternal life depended upon it, **because it does!**" (Spencer W. Kimball, in Conference Report, April 1978, p. 117).[8] (*Search These Commandments*, Melchizedek Priesthood Personal Study Guide, 1984, p. 276)

It is a great comfort to know that the Lord continues to keep a channel of communications open to His Children through the prophet . . . What a blessing it is **to know we have a voice we can trust to declare the will of the Lord**. . . . (Apostle L. Tom Perry, "Prophet Speaks With a 'Voice We Can Trust,'" *Church News* (Oct. 8, 1994)

The words of our living prophets are also accepted as scripture. . . . In addition to these four books of scripture, the inspired words of our living prophets **become scripture** to us. Their words come to us through conferences, Church publications, and instructions to local priesthood leaders. (*Gospel Principles*, pp. 49, 51)

The LDS scripture Doctrine and Covenants 21:4 tells us to give heed to *all* of the prophet's words and commandments. From all these we can see that the words by top leaders of the LDS Church should be taken seriously, and their words and meanings should not be changed.

We Have Prophecy, Archaeological Evidence, and . . .

Many Mormons will present what they think is fulfilled prophecy, archaeological evidence for the Book of Mormon, and historical "facts" as evidence in support of their church. On the surface, many of the items presented appear to be genuine. But an in-depth study demonstrates, as found in chapters 3 to 5 of this book, that in reality such claims are incorrect. Time after time what appears to be evidence in support of Mormonism is in reality a hollow shell of some information, with no substance. As covered in chapter 3 under "Archaeology and the Book of Mormon," one test of "evidence" is: Has it been officially recognized in an official Mormon Church publication?

There Was a Great Apostasy after the Lord Died . . .

The Mormon Church teaches that shortly after the Lord died, a universal apostasy resulted in the loss of "the gospel" of Jesus

Christ on earth. The teachings lost were allegedly restored by Joseph Smith starting with the Book of Mormon and the founding of the Church of Christ in 1830[9] (for more on the name of this church, see "What's in a Name" at the end of chapter 4). In support of this, Mormons will point to Bible verses like the following:

> For I know this, that after my departing shall grievous wolves enter in among you, not sparing the flock. Also of your own selves shall men arise, speaking perverse things, to draw away disciples after them. (Acts 20:29–30)

> And many false prophets shall rise, and shall deceive many. (Matt. 24:11)

They will also likely quote Amos 8:11, Romans 16:17–18, 2 Corinthians 2:17, 2 Peter 2:1, and 1 Timothy 4:1. What Mormons fail to point out is that none of these verses, or any others, say the apostasy would be one hundred percent or universal. We would have to believe that the Holy Spirit was a failure (John 14:26, 16:13; Acts 1:8) and that the apostles the Lord appointed, and then their disciples, and so on were all complete and dismal failures. These ideas are illogical. There is no evidence at all of a universal apostasy shortly after the Lord died. Mormons also fail to mention the many verses that assure Christians that such an apostasy would not happen. For example, we have the Lord's promise in the following:

> And I say also unto thee, That thou art Peter, and upon this rock I will build my church; **and the gates of hell shall not prevail against it.** (Matt. 16:18)

> Heaven and earth shall pass away, **but my words shall not pass away.** (Matt. 24:35)

> For **where two or three are gathered together in my name, there am I in the midst of them.** (Matt. 18:20)

Mormons also ignore their own Doctrine and Covenants 7:1–8, which says that the Apostle John would not die. If this is the case (for which there is no evidence), then he had all the necessary authority to continue the Lord's church. Brigham Young said that so long as one person with authority was alive, the Lord's church would also be.[10]

Where Do You Get Your Authority?

Priesthood authority, the authority to act in God's name, is very important, especially for LDS men. They will frequently ask, "Where do you get your authority?" For a born-again Christian, the answer is found in the Bible:

> Ye also, as lively stones, are built up a spiritual house, **an holy priesthood,** to offer up spiritual sacrifices, acceptable to God by Jesus Christ. . . . **But ye are a chosen generation, a royal priesthood,** an holy nation, a peculiar people; that ye should show forth the praises of him who hath called you out of darkness into his marvellous light. (1 Peter 2:5, 9)

> But as many as received him, **to them gave he power** to become the sons of God, even to them that believe on his name. (John 1:12)

From the following, we learn that our foundation and head is our Lord Jesus Christ, not a worldly man or organization:

> For other foundation can no man lay than that is laid, which is Jesus Christ. (1 Cor. 3:11)

> But I would have you know, that the head of every man is Christ; and the head of the woman is the man; and the head of Christ is God. (1 Cor. 11:3)

From Hebrews 1:1–2 we learn that although in the past we were led by prophets, in these last days we are spoken to and led by Jesus Christ.

Is the Bible Reliable According to the Mormon Church?

When the subject is first discussed, many Mormons will profess acceptance of the Bible. In statements for public consumption, Mormon leaders have suggested the use of the Bible to evaluate the teachings of their Church:

> I say to the whole world, receive the truth, no matter who presents it to you. **Take up the Bible,** compare the religion of the Latter-day Saints with it, and see if it will stand the test. (President Brigham Young, May 1873, *Journal of Discourses* 16:46)

> If Joseph Smith was a deceiver, . . . then he should be exposed; his claims should be refuted, and his doctrines shown to be false, . . . If his claims and declarations were built upon fraud and deceit, there would appear many errors and contradictions, which would be easy to detect. The doctrines of false teachers will not stand the test **when tried by the accepted standards of measurement, the scriptures."** (Apostle Joseph Fielding Smith, *Doctrines of Salvation*, 1954, 1:188)

> . . . convince us of our errors of doctrine, if we have any, by reason, by logical arguments, or by **the word of God, . . .**" (Apostle Orson Pratt, *The Seer,* Jan. 1853, p. 15)

However, do Mormon leaders really view the Bible as an authority higher than their Church and its unique scriptures? It is important to know the true position of the Mormon Church relative to the confidence you can have in the Bible. You are not likely to find out clearly from its missionaries that come to your door, or from your Mormon friend or relative, if you ask about their view of the Bible. But their view will become obvious when you start to challenge LDS teachings and the reliability of the Book of Mormon, Doctrine and Covenants, and Pearl of Great Price (there is more on this below).

The Mormon Church, in its general public statements about the Bible today, usually cites its own *Articles of Faith:*

We believe the Bible to be the word of God as far as it is translated correctly; . . . (*Articles of Faith* #8 in the Pearl of Great Price)

Christians should not have any difficulty with this statement, for there are indeed some truly poor and bad translations. The Jehovah's Witness's *New World Translation of the Holy Scriptures* is one example.[11] But is this what the Mormons really have in mind? In examining this question, we will let top LDS leaders speak for themselves.

Speaking more frankly to their own members, recent Mormon leaders have expressed themselves this way:

> The most reliable way to measure the accuracy of any biblical passage is not by comparing different texts, but by comparison with the Book of Mormon and modern-day revelations. (Letter from the First Presidency [Presidents Benson, Hinckley, and Monson] dated May 22, 1992, to all members of the Church)[12]

Thus, instead of using the Bible to evaluate Mormonism, they would reverse this and use Mormonism to judge the Bible. When speaking frankly, Mormon leaders view the Book of Mormon as more reliable than the Bible:

> Unlike the Bible, which passed through generations of copyists, translators, and corrupt religionists who tampered with the text, the Book of Mormon came from writer to reader in just one inspired step of translation. (President Ezra Taft Benson, "The Keystone of Our Religion," *Ensign* [Jan. 1992]: 5)

The Book of Mormon itself claims that important parts of the Bible have been removed:

> And after they go forth by the hand of the twelve apostles of the Lamb, from the Jews unto the Gentiles, thou seest the formation of a great and abominable church, which is most abominable above all other churches; for behold, they have **taken away** from the gospel of the Lamb many parts which are plain and most precious; and also many covenants of the Lord have they taken away. . . . because of the plain and most precious parts of the gospel of

the Lamb which have been **kept back** by that abominable church, whose formation thou hast seen . . . because of the most plain and precious parts of the gospel of the Lamb which have been **kept back** by that abominable church, which is the mother of harlots, saith the Lamb. . . . (1 Nephi 13:26, 32, 34; also see 2 Nephi 29:2–3, 6–8)

In view of this, the challenge by the top Mormon leaders (quoted first above) to compare Mormonism to the Bible would only make sense if we assume they were addressing non-Mormons. Brigham Young said to use the Bible, Joseph Fielding Smith said the scriptures, and Orson Pratt said the word of God. They are saying that if you compare the teachings of the Mormon Church, you will find them in the Bible. Why would they make such a challenge in the light of the Book of Mormon references that they should have known? Most Mormons, including the ones in 1853, 1873, and 1954, consider the Bible to have parts missing or to be translated wrongly. Were these Mormon leaders just making verbal "smoke" to sound good for their audience? We believe so. Like the various official denials of Mormon polygamy during the time of its early and late practice (about 1835 through 1851 and 1890 through about 1905), such statements were made to improve public relations rather than to express their true feelings.

The Bible Is Loaded with Errors . . .

In their effort to explain away problems (see chapters 3–5 for examples) with their unique scriptures (Book of Mormon, Doctrine and Covenants, Pearl of Great Price) and teachings, Mormons will often point to alleged problems with the Bible. Their logic is that if the Bible can have problems, then it is acceptable for their teachings and other scriptures to have problems. These people are using the wrong standard for comparison. They should first be shown that the Mormon Church considers the Bible to be unreliable in contrast to their unique scriptures (see "Is The Bible Reliable According to Mormonism?" just above). Ask:

"Why would you want to use what your church teaches is a defective document?" They should be walked through the claims of the Mormon Church as illustrated in appendix 1 (Claims to Be the One True Church), appendix 4 (Standards for Following the Top Leaders), and appendix 5 (Standards for Judging Mormon Scriptures). These are the standards for comparison we all should be using.

Answering Questions and Objections from Mormons

While witnessing to people involved with Mormonism, you will be asked a variety of questions. Some will be seeking clarification, some will be used to counter what you said, some will be used just to test you, and some to create confusion. But whatever the reason, experience has identified certain questions that can be expected. While it is not possible to cover all of them, we will help you respond to the ones most frequently asked. The answers will be brief and to the point. We will use the initial **Q** for the LDS question and the initial **A** for the answer. After answering these questions from Mormons, we will arm you with questions you may ask them. Note, if you don't know the answer to a question, say so. Then go and do your homework. Allow the Mormon the same privilege.

1. **Q** God's true Church has prophets and apostles. Does your church have them?
   A First Corinthians 12:28 and Ephesians 2:20, 4:11–19 speak about apostles first and then prophets, so why does the Mormon Church place prophets above apostles? Also, from 1 Corinthians 3:11 we learn that Jesus Christ is our foundation, not men. From Hebrews 1:1–2 we learn that we are no longer led by prophets, but by Jesus!
2. **Q** We Mormon men have the priesthood. Where do you get your authority?
   A Christians get their authority from their faith in Jesus Christ. We learn from Galatians 3:26, 4:4–6 and Romans 8:14 that we are children by adoption; from John 1:12 we

learn he has given us power; and from 1 Peter 2:5–9 (and Rev. 1:6) we learn we have a royal priesthood. From Ephesians 6:19–20 we know that we are also ambassadors of Christ.

3. Q Why are there so many Christian denominations? This is just proof of the great apostasy and the need for God to set up his one true church.

   A While the Bible does speak about apostasy and about wolves getting into the flock (Acts 20:29–30, Gal. 1:7–9, 2 Cor. 11:4) nowhere does it say there would be a *complete* apostasy. The variety of Christian denominations is evidence of the health of Christianity. Perhaps you believe they all teach significantly different doctrine? Those that properly use the Bible are all teaching the biblical gospel of Jesus Christ. They all share a core belief. They have separated into denominations primarily because of nonessential issues, such as music, facilities, the role of the pastor, missionary emphasis, use of tongues, type of baptism (immersion or sprinkling), and similar matters. Mormonism in a little over 150 years has over one hundred off-shoots. With that kind of record how can you criticize Christianity? The Lord has set up his church, but it is not a building or a denomination (see Matt. 18:20, Eph. 4:4–5, 12; Col. 1:24; 1 Cor. 12:13–14, 27). It is not a church that will save you—that is, determine where you will spend eternity. It is your relationship with Jesus Christ. (Now give your testimony, tell them what Jesus Christ has done for you. You might ask: "If you were to die now, do you know where you would spend eternity?" See Acts 2:21; 4:12; 16:31–33; John 3:15–16.)

4. Q. Have you prayed about the Book of Mormon? James 1:5 tells us to do this.

   A We should not pray about the Book of Mormon. It would be tempting God; see chapter 2 under "Evaluating Truth—by Feelings or the Bible?"

5. Q The Book of Mormon was prophesied in Ezekiel 37:16. The Book of Mormon is the stick of Ephraim (for Joseph)

and the Bible is the stick of Judah. Isaiah 29:4 tells us that the Book of Mormon will be like a voice out of the ground, and sure enough, the gold plates were found buried in the ground in a stone box.

A First, note that nowhere in the Bible is the word *stick* used for a book, or *book* used for a stick. Now read Ezekiel 37:16 aloud. Carefully note the context. In verses 17, 21–22 we learn *they* are to be joined and become one nation. Although the Book of Mormon and the Bible are sometimes bound together in one book, they are not *one nation*. It should be obvious that verse 16 has a different meaning than the Mormon interpretation. Isaiah 29:4 speaks of a *familiar spirit*. Letting the Bible interpret itself, we find in Leviticus 19:31 and 20:6 that familiar spirits should be avoided, not sought after.

6. Q In John 10:16 we learn that the Lord has *other sheep* than Israel. This is why Jesus visited the New World.

   A The *other sheep* spoken of by Jesus Christ in John 10:16 are the Gentiles. For more on this, see "The Second Coming" in chapter 5. Also see pages 73–75 of *Mormons Answered Verse by Verse* by Reed and Farkas.

7. Q We believe that people should work for God for free, and that is what we do. Why do Protestant pastors take pay?

   A The Bible says it is okay to accept pay for working for God; see chapter 4, in "Pay for God's Workers."

8. Q We know from Matthew 5:48 ("Be ye therefore perfect, even as your Father which is in heaven is perfect") that we may become like God. Don't you agree?

   A No, I don't agree; see chapter 5, in "Perfection and Salvation."

9. Q We are all brothers and sisters in the Lord, and he has given us a way to return to him.

   A We are not all brothers and sisters in the Lord, but some of us are; see Galatians 3:26; Romans 8:14; John 1:12.

10. Q But I have a testimony. I know the Mormon Church is true. I have good feelings about it.

    A People in various non-Christian churches also have a testimony, but does that make them correct? Feelings are not the method for measuring truth; see chapter 2, in "Evaluating Truth—by Feelings or the Bible?"

11. **Q** We should only say good things about each other. Why are you persecuting us? We don't attack your church.

    A Sometimes we have to reprove, rebuke, and stand up for our faith (2 Tim. 4:2–3, Jude 1:3). Mormons have claimed persecution almost from its beginning. What they seem to ignore is that they had to leave Palmyra, New York; Kirtland, Ohio; Independence, Missouri and the Nauvoo, Illinois area. What do these four widely separated locations have in common with each other? The Mormons themselves! It does not seem reasonable to simply declare that each of the areas had a large core of evil people. And they almost left the Salt Lake City area too.

    The subject of Mormon persecution is very complex. It must include a consideration of economic power, political power, incitement by the Mormons, persecution by the Mormons, persecution by the non-Mormons, and retaliation by both. It is not a simple subject, and to express that the Mormons were persecuted is to pass on an old myth. Until a definitive study is completed, the best that can be fairly said is that there was a conflict of cultures caused by both the Mormons and non-Mormons.[13] The start of this chapter provides more detail; see "We Don't Attack You And Your Church . . ." and question 17 below.

12. **Q** You believe there are three Gods in one body. Who was Jesus Christ praying to in the Garden of Gethsemane? Himself? Is he a ventriloquist?

    A These questions result from a lack of understanding of what Christians believe about the concept called the Trinity. The Mormon should be provided with a correct description of the Trinity (see appendix 3 for the historic definition of the Trinity). They should also be reminded that God is a God of miracles and is omnipresent in person (see Jer. 23:24; Matt. 18:20; Ps. 139:7–10).

13. **Q** Doesn't the fact that there are so many translations of the Bible prove that it is not reliable?

A This question is based on a great deal of ignorance about why there are various translations. The primary drivers for Bible translations are the major changes that have occurred in our culture and language. Our understanding of word meanings has changed significantly in the past two hundred years. At the same time, biblical scholars have gained a better understanding of the biblical languages. The net result is that new Bible translations are needed if we are to continue to refine our understanding of the Bible's message. There is more on this subject at the beginning of chapter 3 under "Why the Bible Is Reliable."

14. **Q** Look at how many Mormons there are. Surely 9 million people can't be wrong?

    A Yes, 9 million people can be wrong, just as easily as Mormons say billions of Catholics and Protestants are wrong or billions of Muslims are wrong. Numbers have nothing to do with right or wrong. Remember our Lord Jesus Christ said "Strait is the gate, and narrow is the way, which leadeth unto life, and few there be that find it" (Matt. 7:14).

15. **Q** Why don't you just teach what you believe and not attack Mormons?

    A The answer to this is found in chapter 1 "What the Bible Says about Witnessing" and at the start of this chapter, "We Don't Attack You and Your Church . . ."

16. **Q** The Bible says "ye shall know them by their fruits." Look at all the great fruits of Mormonism. Isn't this evidence of our truth?

    A First, examine the fruits of Mormonism—the changed and non-Christian teachings about the Father and Son, polygamy, false prophecy, blood atonement, the variety of First Vision stories—some of the items in chapters 3–5. Contrast these with the fruits that the Bible speaks of in 2 Peter 1:2–11 and Galatians 5:22–23.

17. **Q** What you call an attack in *Joseph Smith—History,* 1:18–20 really applied to that day (1820), not to our time. You just don't really understand what is being said.

A Some Mormons are embarrassed by the harshness of *Joseph Smith—History,* 1:18–20. In an effort to mitigate its harshness, some will take various approaches. Some will say that the First Vision only applied to the 1820 period, but not to our time. The Mormon Church has not sanctioned this idea, so we are only dealing with personal opinion.

There is no internal evidence in the First Vision story that supports this idea, but there is evidence that proves it wrong. *Joseph Smith—History,* 1:19 says that the creeds of the sects were an abomination. The creeds of the Methodist and Presbyterian churches (JS-H 1:5, 8–10 names the churches) are essentially the same now as they were in 1820. Although the Baptist Church does not use formal creeds, its founding document (in 1800) said salvation is by the grace of God. The modern continuation of this church still adheres to this same belief.[14] If the creeds and beliefs of the churches in 1820 are essentially unchanged today, it seems logical that if they were an abomination in 1820, they would also be an abomination today. There is nothing published by the Mormon Church that would contradict this idea.

Another approach Mormons use is to say that the "professors" mentioned in *Joseph Smith—History,* 1:19 are "public teachers or college professors." To say that "professors" were teachers is not consistent with (a) the context of its use in *Joseph Smith—History,* 1:19, 22 and 75; (b) the 1820 period dictionary meaning of the word; and (c) the schools in the Palmyra area in the spring of 1820.

The context is the local churches and their creeds. The key thoughts in verses 18 and 19 (up to the word *professor*) are:

1. Joseph Smith asks "which of all the sects was right." (These sects are the local churches mentioned in verses 5, 8–10.)
2. Joseph is told he should join none of them, as they were all wrong.
3. The creeds of these churches were an abomination in God's sight.

We should also consider the meaning of *professor* in dictionaries of the 1820 period. The first definition of *professor* in three dictionaries of the period is: "One who makes open declaration of his sentiments or opinions; particularly, one who makes a public avowal of his belief in the Scriptures and his faith in Christ, and thus unites himself to the visible church" (*An American Dictionary of the English Language* by Noah Webster, 1828); "One who declares himself of any opinion or party" (*A Dictionary of the English Language* by Samuel Johnson, 1805); and "One who declares himself of any opinion or party" (*A Dictionary of the English Language,* abridged by the editor from that of Dr. Samuel Johnson, as edited by Robert Gordon Latham, 1876). A *professor* then in the context of *Joseph Smith—History,* 1:19, 22 and 75, is one who accepts (professes belief in) the creeds that were allegedly an abomination in God's sight. It is they who were teaching "commandments of men."

Many Mormons only give the second dictionary meaning of *professor:* "One that publicly teaches any science or branch of learning; particularly an officer in a university, college or other seminary"; "One who publickly (sic) practises (sic) or teaches an art"; and "One who publicly practises (sic), or teaches, an art . . . One who is visibly religious."

The second dictionary definition is not consistent with the schools in the Palmyra area in the spring of 1820. It was a newly settled area, and the schools were not sophisticated enough to have *professors* teaching at a college, university, seminary level or teaching an art. Milton V. Backman, in his book *Joseph-Smith's First Vision,*[15] reports:

> In the **summer** of 1820 [after Joseph Smith's First Vision] an academy was opened in Palmyra village where students studied Latin and Greek. Four years later an independent school was also established there and pupils gathered in the upper room of the academy where they were taught geography, mathematics, astronomy, surveying, grammar, reading, and writing. (p. 51)

The schools in the spring of 1820 were one-room schoolhouses teaching the basics—reading, writing and arithmetic, not church creeds.

To assume that the meaning of *professor* is the second dictionary definition is inconsistent with the reality of schools in the Palmyra area in the spring of 1820 and with the context of verses 1:5, 8–10, 18–19, 22 and 75. It is clear that the *professors* in *Joseph Smith—History* were those who professed to (accepted) the creeds of the Palmyra churches (sects) Joseph Smith was praying about.

Questions for Mormons

A good way to provoke thought in the person you are witnessing to is to ask questions. But you should generally only ask questions to which you already know the answers. Most of the following have been tested in actual face-to-face discussions with Mormons. The initial **Q** is for the question you may ask, **A** is for the factual answer.

1. **Q** Is it correct that the Mormon Church claims it is God's one and only true church and all others are wrong? (You may wish to combine this item with the next question)
   A Yes, it does claim to be God's one true church. See appendix 1. Other evidence of this is found in the fact that the Mormon Church will not recognize the baptisms performed by other churches.
2. **Q** Is it correct that the Mormon Church claims to be a restoration of God's one true church? Please show me in the Bible where it says there was a complete apostasy and therefore a restoration was needed.
   A While the Bible does teach that wolves would come into the flock and there would be a falling away, it never says there would be a *complete* apostasy as taught by the Mormon Church (Amos 8:11; Matt. 24:11; Acts 20:29–30; Rom. 16:17–18; 2 Cor. 2:17; 2 Cor. 11:4; Gal. 1:7–9; 1 Tim. 4:1; Jude 1:17–19). Matthew 16:18; 18:20; 24:35; 28:20;

and John 10:29; 14:26; 16:13; 17:14, 20 tell me there was not a complete apostasy. We just cannot imagine the Lord's prayer for us in John 17:20 being ignored for nearly seventeen hundred years until Joseph Smith came along, or the Apostle Paul telling us in Ephesians 6:17 to take up a defective sword (the Bible). If there were a complete apostasy, then the Lord's apostles and disciples and the people they appointed to take their place bungled the job. In addition, the Holy Spirit would also have to be a complete bungler, because he had the job (John 14:26; 16:7) to teach and guide. Doctrine and Covenants 7 says that the Apostle John never died. With his living, according to the Mormon Church, the priesthood was not taken away. Was he then a bungler also?

3. **Q** Does the Mormon Church teach that God the Father has a body of flesh and bones? How did he get his body? (Consider using questions 3 to 5 in sequence or combined.)

   A Yes, it does. See Doctrine and Covenants 130:22. Mormonism teaches that God the Father has a father, was once a man like you and me, and progressed to become a God (*Teachings of the Prophet Joseph Smith*, pp. 345–346, 370; *Doctrines of Salvation* 2:47).

4. **Q** Is God the Father the God of the whole creation (the universe), or just of this world?

   A The Mormon Church teaches that God the Father is the God of the universe (see *Gospel Principles*, p. 5 [pre–1989 edition]). Most Mormons will know the Mormon Church's teachings on this and may even know that the Church teaches that God the Father has a father (*Teachings of the Prophet Joseph Smith*, p. 373). Now ask: "If God the Father is God of the whole universe, then what is his father God of?" In evaluating the answer, keep in mind that there is nothing outside of *all creation,* that there is only *one* universe. Some may then say, "Well, God the Father is the God of this world." Then show them Hebrews 1:2 ("made the worlds") and Nehemiah 9:6 ("heaven and heaven of heavens and all their host"). We also know from Isaiah 43:10;

44:6, 8, 24 that there is only *one* God. And from Psalms 90:2; 93:2; Deuteronomy 33:27; Hebrews 13:8 we learn that he has always been God!

5. **Q** Has the Mormon Jesus Christ always been God in the eternity past? If not, when did he become one? Is he the spirit brother of Lucifer? A similar question can be asked about God the Father. See the answer to question 3 above.
   A No, the Mormon Jesus Christ has not always been God according to *Gospel Principles,* page 9 and D&C 93:11–16. As in question 3 above, when God the Father was a man, the spirit of Jesus Christ did not exist! Mormons do not know when he became a God. Yes, he is the spirit brother of Lucifer according to *Gospel Principles* (pp. 9 and 15 pre–1989 edition) and *Gospel Through the Ages* (p. 15). But from Colossians 1:16 we learn that Jesus made everything, which must include the angel who fell and became Lucifer.

6. **Q** I believe Jesus Christ is my Lord and Savior, and to the best I can, I am obedient to his gospel. Why do I need what the Mormon Church teaches?
   A You don't need anything more; see John 5:24; 6:47, 54; 1 John 5:13; Romans 6:23; 2 Timothy 1:9!

7. **Q** As Jesus said in Matthew 5:48 (also found in JST Matt. 5:50), have you become perfect like God the Father?
   A See "Perfection and Salvation" in chapter 5.

8. **Q** Does the Mormon Church teach that Jesus Christ is married?
   A Yes, according to early LDS teachings Jesus was married; see "Is Jesus Married?" in chapter 3.

9. **Q** What is the fulness of the everlasting gospel according to the Mormon Church and some of its top leaders? According to the Mormon Church, is it found in the Book of Mormon and the Bible?
   A It is that information and priesthood from God, which if we accept and live by it, will allow us to reach exaltation in the celestial kingdom (becoming a God). Yes, according to Mormonism, it *supposedly* is found in the Bible and the

Book of Mormon (see the first paragraph of the *Introduction* of the Book of Mormon and D&C 20:9; 42:12; JS-H 1:34). But in reality it is not in the Book of Mormon. For what is missing from the Book of Mormon, see chapter 3, in "What The Mormons Don't Tell Potential Converts."

10. **Q** If you were to die right now, would you spend eternity with God in the celestial kingdom?
 A Yes, if the real biblical Jesus Christ is your Lord and Savior (John 5:24; 6:47; 1 John 5:13; Rom. 6:23; 1 Cor. 1:18; 2 Tim. 1:9).

11. **Q** When you die and go to spend eternity with God in the Celestial Kingdom, if you are stopped at the gates and asked: "Give me one reason why I should let you in?" what would you say?
 A As one Christian pastor correctly said, "Because I'm a member of the family" (as in Gal. 3:26; 4:4–6; Rom. 8:14; John 1:12); or you might say, if it applied to you, "Jesus Christ is my Lord and Savior and his blood has washed me clean of all sin."

12. **Q** Questions to ask if asked to pray about the Book of Mormon:
 a. Which Book of Mormon do you want me to pray about?
 b. Are there some things we should not pray about?
 c. Before we go into that, please tell me if the Book of Mormon contains the fulness of the everlasting gospel (see Q 9 above)?
 A Your second response, in the same order, could be:
 a. The 1830 edition or the present 1981 edition?
 b. Yes, those things that God has already clearly spoken about. We don't tempt God (see chapter 2 in "Evaluating Truth—by Feelings or the Bible?")
 c. Most will not know what the fulness of the everlasting gospel is until you explain it (see Q 9 above).

13. **Q** When at a Mormon temple for a public open house:
 a. Where are the animals kept?
 b. Where are the animal sacrifices done and who does them?
 c. Where is the Holy-of-Holies?

d. Where is the temple veil?

e. Why are there locks on the locker doors?

f. Can all Mormons enter this temple? Why not?

g. Why are the temple activities so secret? In Luke 8:10, 17 Jesus said nothing is secret, nothing is hid.

A a., b., c., They do not exist. The purpose of these questions are to show that LDS temples are not like the one the Jews had in Jerusalem.

d. It is behind the curtain of each endowment room.

e. Because things are stolen in the temple, even though only "honest" Mormons are allowed into the temple.

f. No, only about 20% of the Mormons qualify for a temple recommend.

g. Mormons will tell you that they are sacred not secret—to which you can respond by asking for a detailed description of one.

14. **Q** Does the Mormon Church teach that Mormon men and women have the potential to progress to become Gods, just like God the Father? Please show me where this teaching is found in the Book of Mormon.

    A Yes, see *Gospel Principles*, pages 289–292. It isn't in the Book of Mormon.

15. **Q** Can a Mormon prophet of God remain a prophet even if one of his prophecies fails to come to pass? Would Deuteronomy 18:20–22, 13:1–5 apply?

    A Not according to the Deuteronomy references. See chapter 4 in "False Prophecy, Changes, and Contradictions . . ." and *How To Rescue Your Loved One from Mormonism*, pages 101–112 for examples of false prophecy.

16. **Q** On a given subject, can God reveal to an LDS prophet one thing about himself, and to the same prophet, or another LDS prophet, something totally contradictory on the same subject?

    A The Mormon God allegedly has (see chapter 3)! For one example, see Joseph Smith's King Follet Discourse at the April 1844 General Conference, where he said: "We have imagined and supposed that God was God from all eternity, I will refute that idea. . . ." (*Teachings of the Prophet Joseph Smith,* pp. 345–347; *History of the Church* 6:305; *Journal of Discourses* 6:3). Compare this to Mosiah 3:5, 8; 2 Nephi 29:9; D&C 20:12, 17, 28; Moroni 7:22, 8:18; Mormon 8:18; Moses 1:3–6. In 1 Corinthians 14:33 (also see D&C 132:8) we learn that God is not the author of confusion. There is only one logical conclusion!

17. **Q** Besides Joseph Smith, how do you know that God didn't also visit/speak to Mohammed, the leaders of the Watchtower Society (Jehovah's Witnesses), the prophet of the Reorganized Church of Jesus Christ of Latter Day Saints, and other people and groups that claim to have modern-day prophets?

    A We test what we are told, or feel, by comparing it to what God has already told us, his Word, the Holy Bible. All of the people/groups mentioned fail this test!

18. **Q** Does the Mormon Church teach that Elohim is God the Father and Jehovah is the pre-mortal Jesus Christ? Where in Mormon Scriptures does it say this?

    A Yes, they do teach that the Father is Elohim and the pre-mortal Jesus Christ is Jehovah. See "Elohim and Jehovah" in chapter 4. It cannot be found clearly in LDS scripture. Many verses contradict each other.

19. **Q** Is it correct that the Mormon Church teaches that there is a Mother in heaven? Where is this found in LDS scripture?

    A Yes, they teach there is a mother in heaven, the wife of God the Father (see *Gospel Principles,* p. 9 and *Achieving a Celestial Marriage,* pp. 129–132). This teaching is not found in LDS scriptures.

20. **Q** Does the Mormon Church (in Salt Lake City) still practice polygamy? Why did they stop? Wasn't the revelation forever? Does any group still practice it? What Mormon scripture allowed Mormons to practice polygamy and which one condemns it?

    A Polygamy started about 1835 and was officially ended in 1890. See "Polygamy" in chapter 4.

21. **Q** Since 1830, how many offshoots to Mormonism have there been? Name at least one.

   A Over one hundred; the Reorganized Church of Jesus Christ of Latter Day Saints is the largest. Others still active include the Church of Jesus Christ (the Bickertonites) and the Church of Jesus Christ of Latter Day Saints (the Strangites) (see *Divergent Paths of the Restoration,* by Steven L. Shields). This subject should be brought up if the issue of the many Christian denominations is raised by Mormons.

22. **Q** Does the Book of Mormon contain all of the key important doctrines taught by the Mormon Church?

   A No, it does not; see "What the Mormons Don't Tell Prospective Converts" in chapter 3.

23. **Q** Does the Book of Mormon contain, as stated in the first paragraph of its Introduction, the fulness of the everlasting gospel?

   A No, it does not. See "What the Mormons Don't Tell Prospective Converts" in chapter 3 for the teachings of the Mormon Church not found in the Book of Mormon.

24. **Q** Do the LDS missionaries teach all of the major LDS doctrines before they will baptize a person?

   A No, they do not. See "What the Mormons Don't Tell Prospective Converts" in chapter 3.

25. **Q** Are feelings a reliable way to test truth?

   A No, they are not. See "Evaluating Truth—by Feelings or the Bible?" in chapter 2.

26. **Q** Is the Bible reliable according to the Mormon Church?

   A No, it is not. See "Is the Bible Reliable According to the Mormon Church?" in chapter 6.

27. **Q** Has the Mormon Church always taught there are three personages in the Godhead (as in D&C 130:22)?

   A No, it has not. It once taught that there were only two personages. See "A Comparison of Mormon Teachings on the Nature of God" in chapter 3.

28. **Q** According to Mormonism, is the Holy Ghost a personage? Has this always been the case?

A Today's teaching is that the Holy Ghost is a personage. In D&C 130:22 the Holy Ghost is a *personage*, but the Holy Ghost is an *it* in 2 Nephi 32:5; Alma 34:38; 39:6; D&C 88:3. Now the Holy Ghost is officially considered a personage (*Mormon Doctrine*, p. 359).

29. **Q** President Joseph F. Smith (an LDS prophet and president) said:

Our Father Advanced and Progressed Until He Became God
President Joseph Fielding Smith said: 'Our Father in heaven according to the Prophet [Joseph Smith], had a Father, and since there has been a condition of this kind through all eternity, each Father had a Father' (*Doctrines of Salvation*, 2:47). President Joseph F. Smith taught: 'I know that God is a being with body, parts and passions . . . **Man was born of woman; Christ the Savior, was born of woman; and God the Father was born of woman.**'[16]

Note in this quote that it was just not President Joseph Fielding Smith making the statement. He also quoted the Prophet Joseph Smith. Ask: "Who is the God of the father of God the Father? Who made the first planet that the first man[17] lived on as he progressed to become a God? Please show me where it says this in Mormon Scripture."
A Mormons have no answer for this. It illustrates how some of their teachings cannot be found in their scripture. Some Mormons may try to give their own speculations or opinions, but these are not official. For other examples, see the beginning of chapter 4.

Be alert for Mormons who give their personal opinion to your questions and use little or no Mormon Church teachings in disagreeing with or refuting the answers you have been armed with. The material above uses the teachings of the Mormon Church. Refutations, if any, must also use LDS teachings. For more on this, see "It Doesn't Mean That . . ." in chapter 6.

7

Authors' Testimonies

John R. Farkas

It is an early morning late in February 1984. As usual, I am reading the scriptures while eating breakfast. I am in the Book of Mormon, 1 Nephi 18:25. This verse mentions the cow, ox, ass, horse, goat, and wild goat. This morning is a little unusual, though, in that I find myself questioning how some of these animals could have been in the New World. Didn't the experts (historians, paleozoologists) say that full-size horses were not in the New World until the European explorers and settlers arrived? This thought had occurred to me at least once before, I think, while I was investigating the Church of Jesus Christ of Latter-day Saints. But this time the questions stayed with me, and I found myself thinking about other questions that I apparently had suppressed in the past. I now had become teachable and open, a necessary prerequisite to the receiving of productive witnessing.

Starting with the late February period when I questioned the presence of certain animals in the New World, and continuing for about two months, I seldom had a complete night's sleep. Almost every night I woke up to study for one or two hours, in addition to using all of my free time for the same thing. By the end of February, I had shared my doubts with my resident Mormon expert, my born-again Christian wife, Phyllis. In 1975 when I joined the LDS Church, she had become a Christian and started her studies of Mormonism. I had gone on to become the elders quorum president of the Fairport Ward (1981–1984), and in early 1984 of the newly reorganized Rochester 1st Ward, both in the Rochester, New York Stake, while Phyllis became an expert in Mormon studies and acquired a very extensive library. When I asked her for certain information, I almost always had it within minutes.

By March 15 I had made up my mind to leave the Mormon Church. I knew it when I woke up that night and removed my temple garments.[1] I felt free! My drive to study and learn continued, this time to grow in depth and breadth in Mormon studies and about the Bible and Jesus Christ.

On March 20, 1984, I sent Stake President Dale Dallon my letter of resignation. The reasons I noted in my letter were changes in the *Book of Commandments* versus Doctrine and Covenants, changes to the Book of Mormon, conflicts between early and present-day teachings, and the translation of the *Book of Abraham*. I said that "Joseph Smith was a fraud and has pulled off one of the greatest hoaxes ever!" My name was formally taken off the Church rolls at a Church court on May 10, 1984.

How did I get involved with the Mormon Church in the first place? It was my wife's fault, I now say partially in jest. In 1974 when I became concerned about the food supply chain and saw a need to have a long-term supply of food at home, Phyllis said, "The Mormons do that sort of thing. I'll send them a letter in Salt Lake City." Well, she did, and the LDS missionaries brought the answer to us. We both took the missionary lessons. As a result, I joined in July 1975, and Phyllis became a Christian. (Growing up amidst the tug of war between Christian and Mormon parents was hard on our son Alan. Children suffer in such conflicts.)

During that time, I asked a very significant question without realizing how significant it was. I said to Phyllis, "If we are both praying to the same God, how come we are getting different answers?" Now I realize that the Mormon gods are not of the Bible. Mormonism is not biblical Christianity.

When I left the Mormon Church on March 15, 1984, I was left essentially with the beliefs that I had held in 1974 before I joined the Church. I was still a spiritual infant. I believed in a supreme being, a God, but I did not accept the Bible as the Word of God and I did not accept Jesus Christ as his Son and my Savior. I had a desire to know, so I studied the Bible and books about the Bible, associated with Christians, and attended Christian Sunday services and Sunday school. Through this I came to know that the Bible is the Word of God, and I came to know the real Lord Jesus Christ. But even at this point I didn't know I was "saved."

Only after prayerful reading of John 3:16 with my friend Ross Amico—the founder of a group that was to become Berean Christian Ministries, an organization dedicated to exposing cults—did I fully realize the truth of John 3:16 and that I was the "whosoever" mentioned in this verse. The promise that I could claim was the important thing. Ironically, I accepted Jesus in the Palmyra, New York, Christian church that is adjacent to the Mormon chapel where I had been baptized nine years earlier *to the very week*. These are both thirty-five miles from my home; therefore, I believe it was God's wisdom for it to happen there. On Sunday, July 19, 1984, I answered an altar call at a Webster, New York, Christian church and made public my faith in the real Lord Jesus Christ. Now I know of the simplicity and beauty of his gospel.

I also had a drive to share my newfound knowledge and faith with others, both Mormons and non-Mormons. It is interesting that I had never had anything like this drive to share Mormonism with others. I had not been a good member missionary. In fact, in my last four to six months of Church membership, my feeling against missionary work had surfaced. This became evident to me when my bishop attempted to increase missionary activity in our ward, and I only gave him passive support; but I didn't understand it then.

The Mormon people are a great people. They and their church have many characteristics that I found appealing. They are hardworking, conservative, successful, well-organized, and they give great socials. They are good people in a worldly sense and should have the real Jesus Christ of the Bible. Using the Bible, they present some convincing arguments that appear to support their doctrine. It is important for Christians to know the Bible and to know the real Lord Jesus Christ. A weak Christian is no match against the Mormon story; it is very appealing. It is easier to keep people from joining the Mormon Church than to get members out.

Groups like Berean Christian Ministries perform a multifunction service in combating the false non-Christian teachings of the Mormon Church and similar groups. They help to educate Christians, Mormons, and others; they organize activities that individuals could not handle; they provide support for those trying to get out from under the control of Mormonism and similar organizations.

Since about 1986 I have coordinated the Berean Christian Ministries outreach at the Mormon Hill Cumorah Pageant held annually in July near Palmyra, New York. It is the largest outdoor pageant in America, and up to 100,000 people attend each year. Over 13,000 pieces of Christian literature have been distributed there each year.

I am a graduate of the University of Connecticut with a B.S. degree in mechanical engineering, and I am a licensed New York State professional engineer. From 1962 to 1991, I worked at Xerox Corporation as a project engineer and project engineering manager. My wife, Phyllis, is editor of *The Berean Report.*

One of the reasons I share the items in this last paragraph with you is to illustrate that worldly accomplishment and intellectual capability are different from spiritual capability. I have often been asked how an intelligent person could believe Mormon doctrine, and I can understand why the question is asked. But when the Mormon missionaries came to our house, I was a spiritual baby, and they only taught the milk of the Mormon "gospel." The meat comes later. As Hebrews 5:14 says, "But strong meat belongeth to them that are of full age, even those who by reason of use have their senses exercised to discern both good and evil." I was not of "full age." I was not able to discern the real gospel of Jesus Christ from the "gospel" the Mormon missionaries presented.

Through the prayers of concerned Christians, including my wife, who persevered through a rough situation, I became teachable and then "of full age." I hope and pray that the biblical Jesus Christ is your Lord and Savior as he is mine.

David A. Reed

My early religious training was in a big, white Unitarian church in rural New England south of Boston, where, at age fourteen, I concluded that religion was "the opium of the people." Later I went on to Harvard University and found that such atheism was perfectly acceptable there. By the time I was twenty-two, however, I came to realize that godless evolution offered me only a pointless existence in a meaningless universe, followed by a "dead" end. I began to think about God again.

At that time a Jehovah's Witness was assigned to work alongside me at my job, so I began asking him questions about his beliefs. His answers amazed me. It was the first time I had ever heard religious thoughts presented in a tight-knit, logical framework. In no time, I became a very zealous Witness myself; and I remained in the Watchtower organization for thirteen years, serving as a full-time minister and a congregation elder.

I married Penni Scaggs, who was raised in the organization and was also a zealous Witness. Between the two of us, we conducted home Bible studies with dozens of people and brought well over twenty of them into the sect as baptized Jehovah's Witnesses. What interrupted this life of full dedication to the Watchtower Society? In one word, *Jesus*. Let me explain.

When Penni and I were at a large Witness convention, we saw a handful of opposers picketing outside. One of them carried a sign that read, "Read the Bible, Not the *Watchtower.*" We had no sympathy for the picketers, but we did feel convicted by this sign, because we knew that we had been reading Watchtower publications to the exclusion of reading the Bible. Later on, we actually counted up all of the material that the organization expected Jehovah's Witnesses to read. The books, magazines, lessons, and so forth added up to over three thousand pages each

year—compared with less than two hundred pages of Bible reading assigned—and most of that was in the Old Testament. The
majority of Witnesses were so bogged down by the three thousand pages of the organization's literature that they seldom got
around to doing the Bible reading.

After seeing the picket sign, Penni turned to me and said, "We
should be reading the Bible *and* the Watchtower material." I
agreed, so we began doing regular personal Bible reading with
the aim of becoming better Jehovah's Witnesses.

But as we read the New Testament, we became impressed with
Jesus as a person: what he said and did, how he treated people.
We wanted to be his followers. Especially we were struck with
how Jesus responded to the hypocritical religious leaders of the
day, the scribes and Pharisees. I remember reading over and over
again the accounts relating how the Pharisees objected to Jesus'
healing on the Sabbath, his disciples' eating with unwashed hands,
and other details of behavior that violated their traditions. How
I loved Jesus' response: "You hypocrites, Isaiah aptly prophesied
about you, when he said, 'This people honors me with their lips,
yet their heart is far removed from me. It is in vain that they keep
worshiping me, because they teach commands of men as doctrines'" (Matt. 15:7–9, Watchtower's *New World Translation*).

Commands of men as doctrines! That thought stuck in my
mind, and I began to realize that in fulfilling my role as an elder,
I was acting more like a Pharisee than a follower of Jesus. For
example, the elders were the enforcers of all sorts of petty rules
about dress and grooming, and this reminded me of the Pharisees
who condemned Jesus' disciples for eating with unwashed hands.

Grooming was not the real issue, however. For me it was a
question of whose disciple I was. Was I a follower of Jesus, or an
obedient servant to a human hierarchy? The elders who eventually put me on trial knew that that was the real issue too. They
kept asking, "Do you believe that the Watchtower Society is God's
organization? Do you believe that the Society speaks as Jehovah's mouthpiece?"

With the new perspective that I was gaining from Bible reading, it upset me to see the organization elevate itself above Scrip-

ture, as it did when the December 1, 1981, *Watchtower* said: "Jehovah God has also provided his visible organization. . . . Unless we are in touch with this channel of communication that God is using, we will not progress along the road to life, no matter how much Bible reading we do" (p. 27). It really disturbed me to see those men elevate themselves above God's Word. I voiced criticisms at the meetings, but was then blocked from speaking, so I decided to try writing. That's when I started publishing the newsletter *Comments from the Friends*.

The elders wanted to put me on trial for publishing it, but my wife and I simply stopped going to the Kingdom Hall. By that time, most of our former friends there had become quite hostile toward us. One young man called on the phone and threatened to "come over and take care of" me if he got another newsletter. And another Witness actually left a couple of death threats on our answering machine.

It was a great relief to be out from under the oppressive yoke of that organization. But we now had to face the challenge of where to go and what to believe. It takes some time to rethink your entire religious outlook on life. And we had not yet come into fellowship with Christians outside the Jehovah's Witnesses organization.

All Penni and I knew was that we wanted to follow Jesus and that the Bible contained all the information we would need. We were amazed at what we found in prayerfully reading the New Testament over and over again—things we had never appreciated before, like the closeness that the early disciples enjoyed with the risen Lord, the activity of the Holy Spirit in the early church, and Jesus' words about being born again.

All those years that we were Jehovah's Witnesses, the Watchtower had taken us on a guided tour through the Bible. We gained a lot of knowledge about the Old Testament, and we could quote a lot of Scripture, but we never heard the gospel of salvation in Christ. We never learned to depend on Jesus for our salvation and to look to him personally as our Lord. Everything centered around the Watchtower's works program, and people were expected to come to Jehovah God through the organization.

When I realized from reading Romans 8 and John 3 that I needed to be born of the Spirit, I was afraid at first. Jehovah's Witnesses believe that born-again people who claim to have the Holy Spirit are actually possessed by demons. And so I feared that if I prayed out loud to turn my life over to Jesus Christ, some demon might be listening; and the demon might jump in and possess me, pretending to be the Holy Spirit. (Many Jehovah's Witnesses live in constant fear of the demons. Some of our friends would even throw out second-hand furniture and clothing, fearing that the demons could enter their homes through those articles.) But then I read Jesus' words in Luke 11:9–13 (NKJV). In a context where he was teaching about prayer and casting out unclean spirits, Jesus said:

> And I say to you, ask, and it will be given to you; seek, and you will find; knock, and it will be opened to you. For everyone who asks receives, and he who seeks finds, and to him who knocks it will be opened. If a son asks for bread from any of you who is a father, will he give him a stone? Or if he asks for a fish, will he give him a serpent instead of a fish? Or if he asks for an egg, will he offer him a scorpion? If you then, being evil, know how to give good gifts to your children, how much more will your heavenly father give the Holy Spirit to those who ask Him?

I knew, after reading those words, that I could safely ask for Christ's Spirit (Rom. 8:9), without fearing that I would receive a demon. So, in the early morning privacy of our kitchen, I proceeded to confess my need for salvation and to commit my life to Christ.

Penni teaches fifth grade now in a Christian school that has students from about seventeen different churches. She really enjoys it, because she can tie the Scriptures in to all sort of subjects. And I publish *Comments from the Friends* as a quarterly aimed at reaching Jehovah's Witnesses with the gospel and helping Christians who are talking to Jehovah's Witnesses.

Although the thrust of my outreach ministry is toward Jehovah's Witnesses, I also take advantage of opportunities to share the gospel with Mormons and have had numerous conversations with them—on the street when they were canvassing for potential converts, and in my home when I have accepted their offer of a free copy of the Book of Mormon, which they personally deliver as a way to start weekly discussions. My research on Mormonism started out as preparation for such visits by the missionaries.

The most important lesson Penni and I have learned since leaving the Jehovah's Witnesses is that Jesus is not just a historical figure that we read about. He is alive and is actively involved with Christians today, just as he was back in the first century. He personally saves us, teaches us, and leads us. This personal relationship with God through his Son Jesus Christ is wonderful! The individual who knows Jesus and follows him will not even think about following anyone else: "And a stranger will they not follow, but will flee from him: for they know not the voice of strangers. . . . My sheep hear my voice, and I know them, and they follow me: And I give unto them eternal life; and they shall never perish, neither shall any man pluck them out of my hand" (John 10:5, 27, 28).

Appendix 1

The Mormon Church's Claims to Be the One True Church

What follows are quotes by three presidents, one early and two more recent, of the Church of Jesus Christ of Latter-day Saints (the Mormons or LDS), illustrating their claims to be the one and only true church of Jesus Christ on earth. President Brigham Young in 1853 said:

Truly happy is that man, or woman, or that people, who enjoys the privileges of the Gospel of the Son of God, and who know how to appreciate his blessings. **Who is that person, or that people?** We are ready to reply, '**The Latter-day Saints are the only people** on earth, that we have any knowledge of, to whom the everlasting Gospel has been given in these days; they are the **only people who are the heirs to it, with all its blessings and privileges.** Not to our knowledge is there any other people on the face of this globe that enjoy this inestimable blessing.' (July 24, 1853, and February 20, 1853, *Journal of Discourses* 1:309)

President Spencer W. Kimball in 1982 said:

This is the only true church. . . . .This is not a church. This is **the** Church of Jesus Christ. There are churches **of men** all over the land and they have great cathedrals, synagogues, and other houses of worship . . . (*The Teachings of Spencer W. Kimball*, p. 421)

President Ezra Taft Benson in 1988 said:

This is not just another Church. This is not just one of a family of Christian churches. This is **the Church and kingdom of God, the only true Church upon the face of the earth,** according to the Lord's own words (see D&C 1:30). His Church—it bears His name and it is directed under the authority of His priesthood . . . is a message that will save and exalt the souls of the children of men. There is no other way, because **this is the only true message** and **the only true

159

church upon the face of the whole earth. Those are not my words; they are the words of the Lord Jesus Christ as found in the revelations. (D&C 1.) This gospel in its purity, now restored to the earth, . . . *(Teachings of Ezra Taft Benson*, pp. 164–165, 177)

A Mormon scripture says:

And also those [Joseph Smith and others] to whom these commandments were given, might have power to lay the foundation of this church, and to bring it forth out of obscurity and out of darkness, **the only true and living church upon the face of the whole earth,** with which I, the Lord, am well pleased, . . . (1831, Doctrine and Covenants 1:30, a work viewed by Mormons as scripture)

In a booklet published and copyrighted in 1982 by the Corporation of the President of The Church of Jesus Christ of Latter-day Saints, titled *Which Church Is Right,* it was said:

The Lord provided that salvation should come through his gospel, functioning through his church,. . . . But where is there such a church? How will we recognize it when we see it?. . . . **Is there such a church upon the earth? Until 1830 there was not. It had been lost through the falling away. . . . In 1830 the Almighty restored his church to earth again . . . This restored church is known as The Church of Jesus Christ of Latter-day Saints,** with headquarters in Salt Lake City. (p. 17)

In recent years, the Mormon missionaries have not given this message the same emphasis as in the past. However, it has not been changed; it is just not given the strong focus, probably for public relations purposes. Mormons have learned the old adage "You catch more flies with honey than vinegar."

Appendix 2

Brief History of Mormonism

1805   Joseph Smith Jr., the founder of the organization now called the Church of Jesus Christ of Latter-day Saints (the Mormon Church), is born on December 23 in Sharon, Vermont, the fourth child of Lucy Mack and Joseph Smith.

1816   The Smiths move to the Palmyra, New York area (about forty miles east of Rochester).

1820   In the spring, Joseph Smith Jr., at the age of 14, allegedly receives a visit from God the Father and Jesus Christ, who tell him that all churches are wrong, their creeds are an abomination, and the professors of those creeds are corrupt.[1]

1823   In September, the Angel Moroni allegedly visits Joseph in his bedroom three times in one night. These visits are the start of a series of lessons that prepare him for obtaining gold plates that were allegedly buried in Hill Cumorah, just a few miles south of Palmyra, in Manchester, New York.

1826   On March 20, Joseph Smith is brought to trial[2] on charges of money digging, using a "peep stone" to locate buried hidden treasures for hire, according to Court records of Chenango County, State of New York, *People vs Joseph Smith The Glass Looker*.

1827   Joseph allegedly receives from the Angel Moroni the gold plates that were buried in Hill Cumorah. Written on them in "Reformed Egyptian" is the history of a previously unknown New World people. With the help of God, Joseph translates the writing into what is now the Book of Mormon.

1829   On May 15, John the Baptist allegedly appears and bestows the Aaronic Priesthood on Joseph Smith and his scribe Oliver Cowdery as part of the restoration of God's Church on earth—authority that had been lost shortly after Jesus died.

1829   Probably in the summer, as a continuation of the restoration of God's Church, the Apostles Peter, James, and John allegedly bestow upon Joseph and Oliver the Melchizedek Priesthood.

161

1830	The Book of Mormon is printed by the Grandin Print Shop in Palmyra, New York.
1830	On April 6, the Mormon Church is organized with a handful of people as God's one true Church on earth. At this time it is named the Church of Christ.
1831	The Mormon Church moves to Kirtland, Ohio. At its peak in the 1830s, Kirtland reaches a population of some 3,200—about equal to nearby Cleveland.
1832	Mormons start settlements in Missouri.
1833	Joseph Smith, with the leadership of the church, arranges for seventy-one of his alleged revelations from God to be published as the *Book of Commandments,* at Independence, Missouri. Sixty-five of the planned seventy-one revelations, printed prior to the destruction of the press and facilities by church enemies, are preserved by local Mormons.
1834	The name of the Church is changed to the Church of the Latter Day Saints.
1835	About this time the practice of polygamy starts in private, but is publicly denied.
1835	The 1833 *Book of Commandments* is updated with new revelations, and some old ones are modified (with no mention of the fact that they are changed). The resulting work, entitled Doctrine and Covenants, has two parts. The first part is called "Theology on the Doctrine of the Church of the Latter Day Saints" (better known as the "Lectures on Faith").[3] The second part is named "Covenants and Commandments." Section 101:4 forbids the practice of polygamy.
1838	Joseph Smith leaves Kirtland and goes to Far West, Missouri, fleeing the wrath of the law and disgruntled members.
1838	The name of the Church is changed to the Church of Jesus Christ of Latter-day Saints.
1838	About nineteen Mormon men, women, and children are massacred by non-Mormons at Hauns Mill, Missouri.
1838–39	Mormons are driven out of Missouri due to conflicts between them and the non-Mormons.
1839	Settlement of what is to become Nauvoo, Illinois, starts.
1840	The Mormon Church has about 17,000 members.[4]
1842–44	Joseph Smith, John Taylor, and other members of the community deny in the Mormon Church newspaper that polygamy is practiced, even though it is.
1843	A revelation from God that allows the practice of polygamy is allegedly received, but is not formally announced until 1852, is not included in Mormon scripture until 1876, and is not voted on until

	1880. (This is the present-day D&C 132, which says in its heading that Joseph had known the doctrine and principles since 1831.)
1844	The city of Nauvoo, Illinois, with a population of about 12,000, is the second largest in the state after Chicago. Joseph Smith is the mayor and lieutenant-general of the Nauvoo legion.
1844	On June 7, William Law, Joseph Smith's second counselor, publishes *The Nauvoo Expositor,* which exposes the practice of polygamy in Nauvoo and the teaching by Joseph Smith that there is more than one God.
1844	On June 10, under the authority of Mayor Smith and the Nauvoo City Council, police led by Smith destroy the press, office, and papers of *The Nauvoo Expositor.*
1844	On June 25, Joseph Smith is arrested for the illegal calling out of the Nauvoo legion and for the destruction of *The Nauvoo Expositor* press and office. Along with John Taylor and Dr. Willard Richards, they are held in the Carthage Jail in Carthage, Illinois. On June 27 a mob attacks the jail, killing Joseph and Hyrum in spite of Joseph's efforts at self-defense with a six-shooter. Two men in the mob are also reported killed.
1846	Brigham Young, the second President of the Mormon Church, leads the Mormon trek to what is then a site in Mexico that will become Salt Lake City, Utah. They arrive there in 1847.
1850	Mormon Church membership numbers about 52,000.
1851	The first edition of the Pearl of Great Price is published. It is added to the Mormon scriptures in 1880.
1852	In August, polygamy is announced publicly for the first time at a public Mormon meeting.
1857	On September 11, a combined force of Indians and Mormon militia led by Mormon Bishop John D. Lee attacks and annihilates a wagon train of 120 non-Mormon men, women, and children in the infamous Mountain Meadows Massacre.
1860	The Reorganized Church of Jesus Christ of Latter-Day Saints is officially established at Amboy, Illinois, with Joseph Smith III as President and Prophet.
1860	Mormon Church membership reaches about 61,000.
1862	The Morill Act prohibiting polygamy is passed by U.S. Congress.
1876	D&C 132, which allows polygamy, is first printed in a volume of Mormon scripture.
1880	In October, D&C 132 on polygamy is first voted on by the Mormon membership.
1882	Congress passes the Edmunds Act providing heavy penalties for practicing polygamy. The practice continues by many in hiding.
1887–90	The Edmunds-Tucker Act dissolves the Mormon Church corporation and seizes its property. A short time later, the Supreme Court

finds it constitutional. Legislation is drafted to disenfranchise all Mormons in Utah.

1890   On September 25, Mormon Church President Wilford Woodruff issues his Manifesto asking Mormons to stop the practice of polygamy. At a Mormon Church General Conference on October 6, this Manifesto, now called Official Declaration—1, is accepted by the general membership as "authoritative and binding." This does not reject the revelation allowing polygamy (D&C 132); it just puts the practice aside.

1890   Mormon Church membership is about 188,000.

1921   The first part of the Doctrine and Covenants, the "Lectures on Faith," is removed quietly without such removal ever being presented to the general membership for a vote.

1950   Mormon Church membership is about 1,111,000.

1967   The original papyri, allegedly written by the hand of the Old Testament Prophet Abraham, and used by Joseph Smith to translate the Mormon scripture *Book of Abraham,* are rediscovered. (The document has since been shown to be an Egyptian funereal text, called a "Book of Breathings," written some 1500 years after Abraham's day.)

1970   Mormon Church membership is about 2,931,000.

1978   On September 30, what is now Official Declaration—2, allowing all worthy males in the Mormon Church to hold the priesthood, is accepted by unanimous vote of the members. (Prior to this, a man with any amount of African blood could not hold the priesthood.)

1980   Mormon Church has about 4,640,000 members.

1995   Mormon Church has 9,340,898 members and 48,631 missionaries in the field.

Appendix 3

Mormon Terminology and Doctrine

Terminology

Aaronic Priesthood This is called the lesser priesthood and is usually held by young men starting at the age of 12 to the age of about 18. It is also held for a short time by men who have just become members.

Adam-God From April 1852 to at least February 1877, LDS Church President Brigham Young clearly taught that Adam of the garden of Eden is the father of our spirits, that Adam is the father of the spirit of Jesus Christ and the literal father of his body, and that Adam is our God. This is not now taught by the Mormon Church, and many Mormons are not aware that it once was; others claim Brigham Young is incorrectly quoted.

Afterlife The Mormon afterlife is divided into four levels. The lowest is hell. Then there are three levels of heaven: the telestial, the terrestrial, and the place where God dwells, the celestial (also called the kingdom of God). The celestial kingdom is also divided, the highest level being exaltation, or becoming a God.

Apostles The Mormon Church claims to have the same organization as the primitive church that Jesus set up. It has twelve apostles, sometimes pointed to as proof of their divine appointment as the one true church. (There are actually fifteen or more Apostles most of the time.) The general practice has been for a new President, who is also an Apostle, to appoint counselors from the Quorum of the Twelve; then the openings left by the President and his counselors are filled, resulting in a total of fifteen.

Bible The King James Version of the Bible is one of the canonized scriptures of the Mormon Church; but it is considered incomplete, incorrectly translated, with parts missing. Joseph Smith rewrote it, but only the Reorganized Church of Jesus Christ of Latter Day Saints regularly uses his version. They call it Joseph Smith's "New Translation" of the Bible. The Mormon Church in Salt Lake City calls it the Joseph Smith Translation (JST). Some of it is featured in the footnotes and appendix of their edition of the King James Bible.

Branch A local Mormon congregation that is not large enough to carry out all the programs of the Mormon Church.

Celestial Kingdom See *Afterlife*.

Chapel A local building where Mormons hold their worship services and other weekly activities.

Elohim The name of God the Father.

Eternal Progression The teaching that each of us has the potential to become a God just as God the Father did. He was once a man capable of physical death, was resurrected, and progressed to become a God. We can take a similar path and get all the power, glory, dominion, and knowledge the Father and Jesus Christ have. We then will be able to procreate spirit children who will worship us as we do God the Father.

Exaltation This means becoming a God, the highest degree attainable in the celestial kingdom. See *Eternal Progression*.

Excommunication The highest disciplinary action that the Church can take against a member. Excommunicated persons lose their membership in the Church.

First Presidency A collective name for the President of the Mormon Church and his counselors, usually two.

General Conference An official meeting held twice a year, early in April and October, for general membership instruction, teaching, and announcements by the top leaders of the Mormon Church.

God Within Mormonism, Gods, angels, people, and devils all have the same nature or substance but are at different stages along the line of progression to Godhood. God the Father was once a man like us, capable of physical death, and he progressed until he became a God. He has a body of flesh and bones, but no blood.

Heaven See *Afterlife*.

Hell A place of torment from which most nonbelievers are resurrected into the telestial kingdom; only a limited number remain in hell forever—the devil and the demons and apostates who consciously reject and work against Mormonism.

Holy Ghost The third God of the Godhead (Father, Son, and Holy Ghost), he is a personage of spirit. He, as the Father and Son, cannot be omnipresent.

Holy Spirit Sometimes another name for the Holy Ghost or the Spirit of the Lord (the spirit of Jesus Christ) or the Spirit of God.

Jehovah The name for the preincarnate Jesus Christ.

Jesus Christ The spirit of Jesus Christ was the first spirit born to God the Father and his wife (Heavenly Mother), and he progressed to become a God under the Father. (The Father is also the literal father of Jesus' body in the exact same way we were begotten by our earthly parents.) He now has a body of flesh and bones, but no blood. He is the spirit brother of Satan, whose spirit was procreated in the same way as Jesus' spirit.

Marriage The Mormon Church teaches two types of marriage. One ends at death. The other is for "time and eternity." If the couple is married in a Mormon temple by someone with authority, it is believed they will stay married in the next life. This kind of marriage is needed if they are to progress, not only as husband and wife, but as God and Goddess capable of procreating spirit children.

Melchizedek Priesthood The higher of two categories of ministry in the LDS Church, assigned primarily to seasoned members over the age of 18, and to males only.

Mother in Heaven The wife of God the Father, the mother of his spirit children.

Polygamy The practice of men having more than one wife was started by Joseph Smith in the early to mid-1830s and ostensibly ended in 1890. It is not now practiced within the Church of Jesus Christ of Latter-day Saints, the Mormon Church headquartered in Salt Lake City, Utah. Members found practicing it are excommunicated. Although the practice was ended, the revelation teaching it is still in Mormon scripture (D&C 132). Some Mormon splinter groups believe the teaching was for eternity and still practice it. These modern-day polygamists (called fundamentalists) number in the 30,000–50,000 range.

Pre-existence The Mormon teaching that our spirits (Mormons and non-Mormons) were procreated in a premortal life by God the Father and our Mother in Heaven, that our spirits were born and raised to maturity before coming to earth to obtain physical bodies, and that the spirit of Jesus Christ was the first one born to our heavenly parents.

Priesthood A category of ministry in the LDS Church open to all worthy males 12 years of age or older, empowering them to act in God's name. See *Aaronic Priesthood* and *Melchizedek Priesthood*.

Prophet The top leader of the Mormon Church is considered not only a Prophet but is also a Seer and Revelator. He has the title "President." He is the only one who can speak for and receive new revelation for the whole church. When the existing Prophet dies, the Apostle with the greatest seniority, the president of the Quorum of the Twelve Apostles, becomes the new President. He can appoint counselors, who receive their authority from him.

Salvation A word that Mormons qualify in one of three ways: *unconditional* or *general* salvation is simply resurrection from the dead, granted to all through Christ's atonement; *conditional* or *individual* salvation involves entering the celestial kingdom through works of Mormonism; *full* salvation means exaltation to become a God as a result of temple ceremonies and other works.

Satan One of the spirit children of God. As a consequence of their rebellion, Satan and his angels cannot have mortal bodies—hence cannot progress.

Scriptures The Mormon Church has four documents it calls canonized scriptures: the Book of Mormon, Doctrine and Covenants, Pearl of Great Price, and the King James Version of the Holy Bible.

Son of God Besides Jesus Christ, all of us are viewed as the children of God, his literal spirit children. This makes us all—Mormons, non-Mormons, Jesus Christ, and Satan—spirit brothers. See *Pre-existence* and *Spirits*.

Spirit Children Nonphysical beings allegedly procreated in the pre-existence by God the Father and his wife. Jesus Christ, and even we ourselves, were supposedly born and raised to maturity as spirits before coming into bodies on this earth. The spirit of Satan was also procreated in this way. This makes Satan and Jesus Christ spirit brothers. Jesus selected a righteous path; Satan selected the opposite.

Stake A group of wards and branches, similar to a Roman Catholic diocese.

Standard Works The four canonized scriptures (see *Scriptures* above) used by the Mormon Church are called the *standard works*.

Temple One of about four dozen large religious buildings around the world in which special ceremonies are performed for the living and the dead; off limits to nonmembers and even to Mormons who lack a "temple recommend" from their leaders.

Trinity This word is used by Christians to summarize the biblical teaching that within the one true God are three persons: God the Father, God the Son, and God the Holy Ghost. They share the same nature or substance, so that there are not three Gods, but three persons in the one God.

Mormons say they also believe in the trinitarian concept of God. But what they really mean is that God the Father is a God, God the Son is another God, and God the Holy Ghost is a third God, and that they are *one God* because they are *one in purpose*. Mormons often have an incorrect understanding of what Christians mean by the Trinity. They usually think Christians believe that the

Father, Son, and Holy Ghost are one person (i.e., Monarchianism) or that God shows himself as the Father or the Son or the Holy Ghost (*i.e.* Modalism).

Virgin Birth A concept negated by the view that God, a resurrected man with flesh and bones according to Mormon teachings, literally fathered Jesus in the flesh in the same way in which earthly men father their children. Many Mormons are unaware of their church's teaching on this subject.

Ward A local Mormon congregation. The building it meets in is called a chapel.

Word of Wisdom The Mormon teaching requiring abstinence from tobacco, alcohol, and hot drinks (interpreted as meaning tea and coffee).

Doctrine

Joseph Smith, the founder and first President of the Mormon Church, said at its April 1844 General Conference, ". . . it is necessary we should understand the character and being of God. . . . It is the first principle of the Gospel to know for a certainty the Character of God. . . ." Brigham Young, the second president of the Mormon Church, said similarly on February 8, 1857: "It is one of the first principles of the doctrine of salvation to become acquainted with our Father and our God."[1] Tell your Mormon contact that you agree that it is important to know and understand the character of God and that you wish, therefore, to look at the nature of God, *i.e.,* the characteristics of God as taught in the LDS scriptures and teaching manuals.

What follows are quotes from publications by the Mormon Church illustrating some of their unique teachings. Mormonism's founder Joseph Smith departed radically from traditional Christianity in his teachings about God:

> God an Exalted Man—I will go back to the beginning before the world was, to show what kind of being God is. What sort of a being was God in the beginning? . . . I am going to tell you how God came to be God. **We have imagined and supposed that God was God from all eternity. I will refute that idea, and take away the veil, so that you may see.** . . . It is the first principle of the Gospel to know for a certainty the Character of God . . . that **he was once a man like us;** yea, that God himself, the Father of us all **dwelt on an earth. . . .** (*Teachings of the Prophet Joseph Smith*, pp. 345–346)[2]

Joseph Fielding Smith took the following from a talk given by Joseph Smith at an official Mormon Church meeting (General Conference) in April 1844. The talk is known as the King Follett Discourse. Mormon teaching manuals expand on this doctrine:

> Our **Father Advanced and Progressed Until He Became God**
> President Joseph Fielding Smith said: "Our Father in heaven according to the Prophet [Joseph Smith], had a Father, and since there has been a condition of this

kind through all eternity, each Father had a Father" (*Doctrines of Salvation*, 2:47). President Joseph F. Smith taught: "I know that God is a being with body, parts and passions. . . . Man was born of woman; Christ the Savior, was born of woman; and God the Father was born of woman."

As shown in this chapter, our Father in heaven was once a man as we are now, capable of physical death . . . he and our mother in heaven were empowered to give birth to spirit children . . . (*Achieving a Celestial Marriage*, p. 132)

Mormon Apostle Orson Pratt taught in the periodical *The Seer*:

We were begotten by our Father in Heaven; the person of our Father in Heaven was begotten on a previous heavenly world by His Father; and again, He was begotten by a still more ancient Father; and so on from generation to generation, from one heavenly world to another more ancient, until our minds are wearied and lost in the multiplicity of generations and successive worlds. . . . (1853, p. 132)

Mormon scripture adds further detail:

The **Father has a body of flesh and bones as tangible as man's;** the Son also; but the Holy Ghost has not a body of flesh and bones, but is a personage of Spirit. Were it not so, the Holy Ghost could not dwell in us. (D&C 130:22, April, 1843)

Note how the above references say that the Father has a body of flesh and bones as tangible as man's, he was once a man like us, he was born of a woman, he dwelt on an earth, he has not always been God, and he had a father.

Appendix 4

Mormon Standards for Following the Words of the Top Mormon Leaders

The first five items below are from *Search These Commandments*, Melchizedek Priesthood Personal Study Guide, published and copyrighted (1984) by the Mormon Church. It is a teaching manual for Mormon men. The sixth item is from a similar 1983 manual titled *Come Follow Me*.

More Than the Advice of Man

Elder George Albert Smith noted: "When we are instructed by the President of this Church, we believe he tells us what the Lord would have us do. **To us it is something more than just the advice of man**" (in Conference Report, Oct. 1930, p. 66). (*Search These Commandments*, p. 272)

We Have Our Marching Orders

President Ezra Taft Benson has said, "Therefore, the most important reading we can do is any of the words of the Prophet contained each week in the Church Section of the *Deseret News* and any words of the Prophet contained each month in our Church magazines. Our **marching orders** for each six months are found in the general conference addresses which are printed in the *Ensign* magazine" ("Fourteen Fundamentals in Following the Prophets," 1980 *Devotional Speeches of the Year*, [Provo, Utah: Brigham Young University Press, 1981], p. 27). (*Search These Commandments*, p. 273)

We Have God's Will for Us

President Ezra Taft Benson has pointed out that "the most important prophet, so far as you and I are concerned, is the one living in our day and age to whom the Lord is currently revealing **His will for us**" ("Fourteen Fundamentals in Following the Prophets," *1980 Devotional Speeches of the Year*

[Provo, Utah: Brigham Young University Press, 1981], p. 27). (*Search These Commandments*, p. 275)

The Lord Will Never Permit Him to Lead Us Astray

President Wilford Woodruff gave the following assurance, "I say . . . the Lord **will never permit** me nor any other man who stands as the President of this Church, to lead you astray" (*The Discourses of Wilford Woodruff*, p. 212). (*Search These Commandments*, p. 276)

Our Eternal Life Depends on His Word

At the conclusion of one General Conference, President Kimball said: "Now as we conclude this general conference, let us all give heed to what was said to us. Let us assume the counsel given applies to *us*, to me. Let us **hearken to those we sustain as prophets and seers, as well as the other brethren, as if our eternal life depended upon it, because it does!**" (Spencer W. Kimball, in Conference Report, Apr. 1978, p. 117; or *Ensign*, May 1978, p. 77). (*Search These Commandments*, p. 276)

Mind, Will, and Voice of the Lord and Power of God unto Salvation

President Harold B. Lee once said at the close of a general conference, "If you want to know what the Lord has for this people at the present time, I would admonish you to get and read the discourses that have been delivered at this conference; for what these brethren[1] have spoken by the power of the Holy Ghost is **the mind of the Lord, the will of the Lord, the voice of the Lord, and the power of God unto salvation**" (in Conference Report, Apr. 1973, p. 176; or *Ensign*, July 1973, p. 121). (*Come Follow Me*, p. 11)

President Woodruff, President Lee, and President Kimball were presidents of the Church when they made these statements. The other three men were apostles, the level just below the president of the Church, when they made the statement, and became the president of the Church at a later date.

Follow the President Even if What He Says Is Wrong

And President Harold B. Lee stated that "President Grant used to say to us . . . 'Brethren, keep your eye on the President of this Church. **If he tells you to do anything and it is wrong and you do it,** the Lord will bless you for it. But you don't need to worry; the Lord will **never** let his mouthpiece lead this people astray." (*Ensign*, October 1972)

When the Leaders Speak, the Thinking Has Been Done

When our leaders speak the thinking has been done. When they propose a plan—it is God's plan. When they point the way, there is no other which is safe. When they give direction, it should mark the end of controversy. (*The Improvement Era*, under "Ward Teacher's Message for June 1945," p. 354; also found in *Deseret News*, Church Section, May 26, 1945, p. 5)

Words of the Living Prophet Become Scripture to Us

The words of our living prophets are also accepted as scripture. . . . In addition to these four books of scripture, the inspired words of our living prophets **become scripture** to us. Their words come to us through conferences, Church publications, and instructions to local priesthood leaders. (*Gospel Principles,* pre-1989 editions, pp. 49, 51)

No One Can Say I Ever Gave Wrong Counsel

I see around me a great people. Joseph Smith was called of God, and sent to lay the foundation of this latter-day kingdom. He presided over this people fourteen years. Then he was martyred. Since that time your humble servant has presided over and counselled this people; . . . For the space of twenty-four years he has watched over their interests, . . . What man or woman on the earth, what spirit in the spirit-world can say truthfully **that I ever gave a wrong word of counsel, or a word of advice that could not be sanctioned by the heavens?** The success which has attended me in my presidency is owing to the blessings and mercy of the Almighty. (President Brigham Young [Dec. 29, 1867], *Journal of Discourses,* 12:127)

I Have Never Preached a Sermon They May Not Call Scripture

The Lord is in our midst. He teaches the people continually. I have **never** yet preached a sermon and sent it out to the children of men, that they may not call **Scripture.** Let me have the privilege of correcting a sermon, and it is as good Scripture as they deserve. The people have the oracles of God continually." (President Brigham Young [Jan. 2, 1870], *Journal of Discourses,* 13:95)

My Words When Approved by Me Are as Good as Scripture

Brother Orson Hyde referred to a few who complained about not getting revelations. I will make a statement here that has been brought against me as a crime, perhaps, or as a fault in my life. Not here, I do not allude to anything of the kind in this place, but in the councils of the nations—that Brigham Young has said "when he sends forth his discourses to the world they may call them Scripture." I say now, when they are copied and approved by me they are as good Scripture as is couched in this Bible, and if you want to read revelation read the sayings of him who knows the mind of God, without any special command to one man to go here, and to another to go yonder, or to do this or that, or to go and settle here or there. (President Brigham Young at General Conference, [Oct. 6, 1870], *Journal of Discourses,* 13:264)

There Is More Scripture Than in the Standard Works

Millions feel that what is written in the Bible is the total of the revelations of the Lord, in spite of John's statement that if all that Jesus did were recorded, there would be numerous books. Some Latter-day Saints also make a similar error and feel that what is written in the *standard works* constitutes the sum total of the revelations in this dispensation. To this error George Q. Cannon, a member of the First Presidency, speaks:

'Some have deceived themselves with the idea that because revelations have not been written and published, therefore, there has been a lessening of power in the Church of Christ. This is a very great mistake. . . . the servants of the Lord **do receive revelations, and they are as binding upon the people as though they were printed and published throughout all the Stakes of Zion.** The oracles of God are here, and He speaks through His servant whom He has chosen to hold the keys. . . . We have been blessed as a people with an abundance of revelation. Have this people ever seen the day when the counsel of God's servants has not been sufficient to guide them in the midst of difficulties? No. We never have. **There has not been a single minute that this people has been left without the voice of God;** there has not been a single minute since this church was founded to this time that the power of God has not been plainly manifested in our midst. . . .' (*Gospel Truth*, p. 332)

The day of revelation has never passed; the Lord continues to communicate with his servants in our own day *as always*. ([President] Spencer W. Kimball, *Faith Precedes the Miracle*, pp. 21–22)

The Lord's Will Also Comes from the Prophet

We are to give heed to the words of eternal life. In other words, we must understand and live by the revelations the Lord has granted to His prophets. These are contained in the four *standard works* **and the written and public declarations of our current prophet.** ("Three Imperative Responsibilities," London England Area Conference, 19–20 June 1976.) *(Teachings of Ezra Taft Benson*, pp. 404–405)

MORMON SCRIPTURES SAY THE FOLLOWING:

Give Heed to All the Prophet's Words and Commandments

Wherefore, meaning the church, thou shalt give heed unto **all** his [the Prophet's] words and commandments which he shall give unto you as he receiveth them, walking in all holiness before me; (April 6, 1830, D&C 21:4)

When Elders Are Moved by the Holy Ghost It Shall Be Scripture

And this is the ensample unto them, that they [the elders, see verse 7] shall speak as they are moved upon by the Holy Ghost. And whatsoever they [the elders] shall speak when moved upon by the Holy Ghost **shall be scripture,** shall be the will of the Lord, shall be the mind of the Lord, shall be the word of the Lord, shall be the voice of the Lord, and the power of God unto salvation. (Nov. 1831, D&C 68:3–4).

The Lord Will Do Nothing without Telling the Prophet

Surely the Lord God will do nothing, but he revealeth his secret unto his servants the prophets. (Amos 3:7)[2]

At times Mormon voices have sounded a cautionary note, calling for current pronouncements to be subjected to the test of being in agreement with the *standard works*. Note the words of President Harold B. Lee and Apostle Joseph Fielding Smith:

Only the President Can Teach Doctrine Not in the Standard Works, But It Cannot Contradict What Is Already There.

> We have the standard Church works. Why do we call them standard? If there is any teacher who teaches a doctrine that can't be substantiated from the standard church works—and I make one qualification, and that is unless that one be the President of the Church, who alone has the right to declare new doctrine—. . . The President of the Church alone may declare the mind and will of God to His people. No officer nor any other church in the world has this high and lofty prerogative. When the President proclaims any such **new doctrine**, he will declare it to be a revelation from the Lord. . . . .
>
> It is not to be thought that every word spoken by the General Authorities is inspired, or that they are moved upon by the Holy Ghost in everything they write. I don't care what his position is, if he writes something or speaks something that goes beyond anything that you can find in the standard church works, **unless** that one be the prophet, seer, and revelator—please note that one exception—you may immediately say, 'Well, that is his own idea.' And if he says something that contradicts what is found in the standard church works, you may know by that same token that it is false, regardless of the position of the man who says it. We can know or have the assurance that they are speaking under inspiration if we so live that we can have a witness that what they are speaking is the word of the Lord. There is only one safety, and that is that we shall live to have the witness to know. President Brigham Young said something to the effect that 'the greatest fear I have is that the people of this Church will accept what we say as the will of the Lord without first praying about it and getting the witness within their own hearts that what we say is the word of the Lord.' ([President] Harold B. Lee, *Stand Ye In Holy Places,* pp. 109–110, 162–163)

It is important to understand this concept taught by President Lee. He is saying that only the President of the Church, the Prophet, can teach new doctrine that is not in the *standard works*. But even his teachings, if they conflict with what is already in them, can be ignored.

Both men seem to agree with each other that new teachings must not conflict with the *standard works*. Consider also these words of Apostle (and later president) Joseph Fielding Smith:

STANDARD WORKS JUDGE TEACHINGS OF ALL MEN. It makes no difference what is written or what **anyone** has said, if what has been said is in conflict with what the Lord has revealed, we can set it aside. My words, and the teaching of **any other** member of the Church, **high or low**, if they do not square with the revelations, we need not accept them. Let us have this matter clear. We have accepted the four *standard works* as the measuring yardsticks, or balances, by which we measure every man's doctrine.

You *cannot accept* the books written by the authorities of the Church as standards in doctrine, *only in so far* as they accord with the revealed word in the standard works. ([Apostle] Joseph Fielding Smith, *Doctrines of Salvation*, 3:203)

ALL TEACHINGS MUST CONFORM TO REVELATIONS. It is not to be supposed from this that all that has been written outside of the standard works of the Church is discarded and rejected, for these things are profitable as helps in the government of the Church, and to promote faith in the members. The point is this, if in these books mistakes are found, 'they are the mistakes of men,' and the Church as an organization is not to be held accountable for them, but for that which is received from time to time by vote of the Church, as it comes through the President of the High Priesthood. When the Lord reveals his mind and will, it is to be received, 'whether by mine own voice or by the voice of my servants, it is the same,' **but we are not to be judged by unauthorized sayings or deeds.** (Apostle Joseph Fielding Smith, *Doctrines of Salvation,* 1:322–323)

These cautionary words concerning new teachings are clearly in the minority—an exception to what other Mormon leaders have traditionally said. Joseph Fielding Smith wrote his remarks at a time (prior to 1956) when he was an apostle, not when he spoke as president (1970–1972). In addition, this view is not supported by LDS scripture and actual past practice, hence is really his own personal opinion. Moreover, even he expressed himself on other occasions in full agreement with the more prevalent view:

WHAT IS SCRIPTURE? When one of the brethren stands before a congregation of the people today, and the inspiration of the Lord is upon him, he speaks that which the Lord would have him speak. It is just as much scripture as anything you will find written in any of these records, and yet we call these the *standard works* of the Church. We depend, of course, upon the guidance of the brethren who are entitled to inspiration. (*Doctrines of Salvation*, 1:186)

All of the above quotes combine to establish the weighty significance Mormons attach to statements by their leaders, particularly statements by LDS Church presidents. This authoritative nature of presidential pronouncements should be kept in mind during discussions with Mormons.

Appendix 5

Mormon Standards for Judging Mormon Scriptures

What Did the Founder of the Mormon Church Say?

Joseph Smith was the founder and first president of the Mormon Church and allegedly received by the power of God over 95 percent of the present-day Mormon scriptures (except for the Bible). Note in the following how he said "there is no error in the revelations which I have taught." In other words, this man, who was responsible for most of the Mormon scriptures, claims they have no errors.

> When did I [the Prophet Joseph Smith, May 1844] ever teach anything wrong from this stand? When was I ever confounded? I want to triumph in Israel before I depart hence and am no more seen. I never told you I was perfect but **there is no error in the revelations** which I have taught. Must I, then, be thrown away as a thing of naught? (*Teachings of the Prophet Joseph Smith*, p. 368)

On another occasion Joseph Smith said his enemies could not strike a blow at the doctrine because it was true, and no man could upset it.

> . . . Why do not my [Joseph Smith's] enemies strike a blow at the doctrine? They cannot do it: **it is truth, and I defy all men to upset it.** (March 1844, *History of the Church*, 6:272)

With regard to the Book of Mormon, Joseph Smith said:

> I told the brethren that the Book of Mormon was the **most correct book on earth**, and the keystone of our religion, and a man would get nearer to God by abiding by its precepts than any other book. (*History of the Church*, 4:461)

In summary, the founder of the Mormon Church and the man responsible for 95 percent of its unique scripture stated very clearly that there were no errors in them.

What Do Mormon Scriptures Say?

The first revelations that the Prophet Joseph Smith allegedly received from God were collected in 1833 into a book called the *Book of Commandments*. Chapter 1, verse 7 (hereafter 1:7) says: "Search these commandments for they are **true and faithful . . .**" A subsequent edition of this book, called Doctrine and Covenants (abbreviated D&C), was published in 1835. Section 1:7 of this edition is *exactly* the same as 1:7 in the *Book of Commandments*. (The present 1986 edition of the D&C has the *exact* wording as that in the 1833 and 1835 editions under 1:7, but it is now numbered 1:37.) If they were "true and faithful" in the 1833 edition, one would expect no changes in the 1835 edition, and the present-day 1986 edition. This is not to say that allowance should not be made for new "revelation." It is the old existing revelations as they first appear in each edition that should be compared to following editions. It seems reasonable to expect that no *differences* would be observed seeing that Joseph Smith said they had no error and revelation allegedly from God also said they "are true and faithful."

Another verse conveys a similar thought:

> For God doth not walk in crooked paths, neither doth he turn to the right hand nor to the left, **neither doth he vary from that which he hath said,** therefore his paths are straight, . . . (July 1828, D&C 3:2)

This was numbered 2:1 in the 1833 edition and 30:1 in the 1835 edition. Moreover, Doctrine and Covenants 42:56 says:

> Thou shalt ask, and my Scriptures shall be given as I have appointed, and **they shall be preserved** in safety.

These all reinforce what Joseph Smith said, namely that no errors should be expected in the revelations and "they shall be preserved."

The Book of Mormon expresses similar ideas. In Alma 41:8 we find: "Now, the decrees of God are **unalterable;** . . ." And in Mormon 9:9 we have: "For do we not read that God is the same yesterday, today, and forever, and in him there is no variableness **neither shadow of changing?**" The Prophet Joseph Smith said the Book of Mormon was "the most correct of any book on earth and the keystone of our religion, and a man would get nearer to God by abiding by its precepts, than by any other book" (*History of the Church*, 4:461). This quote is also found in the Introduction of the Book of Mormon. The title page of the Book of Mormon also says it came ". . . forth by the gift and power of God. . . ." Doctrine and Covenants 17:6 has God saying the Book of Mormon "is true."

Using the Mormon Standards to Examine Mormon Scripture

It seems reasonable, then, to expect a high standard of quality in both content and the transmitted text of the Mormon scriptures. This should also mean no contradiction in teachings, if they are from God, for in 1 Corinthians 14:33 we learn that God is not the author of confusion. If there is confusion, then it seems reasonable it must not be from God.

The Joseph Smith Translation of the Bible

As you read and study the material in this book, keep in mind that we have taken great care not to take the references out of context. We have also consulted the *Joseph Smith Translation* (JST) of the Bible (sometimes called the *Inspired Version* and the *New Translation* by the RLDS) to be sure we were representing Joseph Smith's thoughts in 1833 when he finished it. Joseph Smith said that he started this translation of the Bible at the commandment of the Lord and that on January 10, 1832, he was told to continue the work until it was finished (D&C 73:3–4). On February 2, 1833, Joseph said:

> I completed the translation and review of the **New Testament,** on the 2nd of February, 1833 and sealed it up no more to be opened till it arrived in Zion. (*History of the Church, 1:324*)[1]

On July 2, 1833, Joseph said:

> We this day finished the translating of **the Scriptures,** for which we returned gratitude to our Heavenly Father . . . Having finished the translation of the Bible, a few hours since .. . . (*History of the Church,* 1:368–369)

There is some debate if it was really finished then, but we'll take Joseph at his word, seeing he claimed the Lord commanded him to finish it (D&C 73:3–4) and he said he had completed the New Testament and, later on, the Bible.

We compare the *Joseph Smith Translation* (JST) to the Bible in several places in this book. If indeed the unique Mormon scriptures are what is claimed, then they must be measured by their own standards.

Appendix 6

Recommended Reading and Support Groups

Helpful Books on the Bible and Biblical Christianity

Bruce, F. F. *The Canon of Scripture*. Downers Grove, Ill.: InterVarsity Press, 1988. 349 pages.

———. *The New Testament Documents, Are They Reliable?* Grand Rapids: Eerdmans, 1943–1980. 120 pages.

The Complete Biblical Library. 16 vols. Springfield, Mo.: Gospel Publishing House, 1986.

Lightfoot, Neil R. *How We Got the Bible*. Grand Rapids: Baker, 1963, 1983. 167 pages.

McDowell, Josh. *Evidence That Demands a Verdict*. San Bernardino, Calif.: Campus Crusade for Christ, Inc., 1972. 14th printing, 1977. 387 pages.

———. *More Evidence That Demands a Verdict*. San Bernardino, Calif.: Campus Crusade for Christ, Inc., 1975. 12th printing, 1981. 389 pages.

——— and Larson, Bart. *Jesus, A Biblical Defense of His Deity*. San Bernardino, Calif.: Here's Life Publishers, Inc., 1983. 137 pages.

——— and Stewart, Don. *Answers to Tough Questions*. San Bernardino, Calif.: Here's Life Publishers, Inc., 1980. 197 pages.

———. *Reasons Skeptics Should Consider Christianity*. San Bernardino, Calif.: Campus Crusade for Christ, Inc., 1981. 230 pages.

Morris, Henry M. *The Bible and Modern Science*. Chicago: Moody Bible Institute, 1951, 1968. 137 pages.

Strong's Exhaustive Concordance of the Bible. Nashville/New York: Abingdon Press, 1894. 32nd printing, 1974. About 1,500 pages.

Vine, W. E. *An Expository Dictionary of Biblical Words*. Nashville/Camden/New York: Thomas Nelson Publishers, 1985. About 1,000 pages.

180

Pro-Mormon Publications

Arrington, Leonard J. and Bitton, Davis. *The Mormon Experience.* New York: Vintage Books, 1980.

Gospel Principles. Salt Lake City: The Church of Jesus Christ of Latter-day Saints, 1992. Pre-1986 editions are best.

McConkie, Bruce R. (Apostle). *Mormon Doctrine.* Salt Lake City: Deseret Book Co., 1979 edition.

Richards, LeGrand (Apostle). *A Marvelous Work and a Wonder.* Salt Lake City: Deseret Book Co., 1976, 1979 editions.

Talmage, James E. (Apostle). *The Articles of Faith,* the Church of Jesus Christ of Latter-day Saints, 1987.

Mormon scriptures, the *standard works:* The Holy Bible (King James Version), Book of Mormon, Doctrine and Covenants, Pearl of Great Price.

Critical Works

Those with a star (*) are suitable for the new and maturing student.

Banister, S. I. *For any Latter-day Saint: One Investigator's Unanswered Questions.* Fort Worth: Star Bible Publications, Inc., 1988. Very good selection of copies from Mormon publications.

*Bodine, Jerry and Bodine, Marian. *Witnessing to Mormons.* San Juan Capistrano, Calif.: Christian Research Institute, 1978.

Brodie, Fawn M. *No Man Knows My History.* 2nd ed. New York: Alfred A. Knopf, 1971.

*Cares, Mark J. *Speaking the Truth in Love to Mormons.* Milwaukee: Northwestern Publishing House, 1993. This book is recommended for its 185 pages on Mormon culture and terminology.

Christensen, Culley, M.D. *The Adam-God Maze.* Scottsdale, Ariz.: Independent Publishers, 1981.

Cowan, Marvin W. *Mormon Claims Answered.* Self-published, Salt Lake City, 1984 and 1989. Also available in Spanish.

*Farkas, John R. and Reed, David A. *Mormonism—Changes, Contradictions and Errors.* Grand Rapids: Baker, 1995.

*Geer, Thelma "Granny." *Mormonism, Mama, and Me.* Chicago: Moody Press, 1986.

Larson, Charles M. *By His Own Hand Upon Papyrus.* Grand Rapids: Institute for Religious Research, 1985. Rev. 1992.

*McElveen, Floyd. *God's Word, Final, Infallible and Forever.* Grand Rapids: Gospel Truths Ministries, 1985.

*McKeever, Bill. *Answering Mormon's Questions.* Minneapolis: Bethany House, 1991.

——— and Johnson, Eric. *Questions to Ask Your Mormon Friend.* Minneapolis: Bethany House, 1994.

*Reed, David A. and Farkas, John R. *How to Rescue Your Loved One from Mormonism.* Grand Rapids: Baker, 1994.

*————. *Mormons Answered Verse by Verse*. Grand Rapids: Baker, 1992.

*Rhodes, Ron and Bodine, Marian. *Reasoning From the Scriptures With the Mormons*. Eugene, Ore.: Harvest House, 1995.

*Scott, Letayne C. *Ex-Mormons: Why We Left*. Grand Rapids: Baker, 1990.

Spencer, James R. *Beyond Mormonism, An Elder's Story*. Grand Rapids: Chosen Books, 1984.

Tanner, Jerald and Tanner, Sandra. *3,913 Changes in the Book of Mormon*. Salt Lake City: Utah Lighthouse Ministry, no date. A photo reprint of the original 1830 edition of the Book of Mormon with all the changes marked to show different readings in the 1962 edition.

————. *The Changing World of Mormonism*. Chicago: Moody Press, 1980. This is a condensed version of *Mormonism—Shadow or Reality?*

————. *Mormonism—Shadow or Reality?* 5th ed. Salt Lake City: Utah Lighthouse Ministry, 1987. In our opinion this is the single best research book on what is wrong with Mormonism.

Thalson, Craig L. *Adam-God*. Payson, Utah: Publishment, 1991.

Van Wagoner, Richard S. *Mormon Polygamy—A History*. Salt Lake City: Signature Books, 1986.

*Witte, Bob. *Where Does It Say That?* Grand Rapids: Gospel Truths Ministries, no date. Good selection of copies from Mormon publications.

Note: There are many other excellent books on Mormonism and cults in general. Those listed above are some that we believe the average reader will find most helpful. A number of other useful books, booklets, and newsletters have been self-published by the various ministries noted below.

Ministries and Support Groups

Alpha & Omega Ministries, P.O. Box 47041, Phoenix, AZ 85086

Berean Christian Ministries, P.O. Box 1091, Webster, NY 14580; Phone (716) 872–4033, 8:00 A.M. to 8:00 P.M. eastern standard time. This is the ministry of John R. Farkas, an ex-Mormon and one of the authors of this book. E-mail address: bcmmin@frontiernet.net Our web page: http://www.frontiernet.net/~bcmmin

Christian Research Institute, P.O. Box 500, San Juan Capistrano, CA 92693

Comments from the Friends, P.O. Box 819, Assonet, MA 02702. This is the ministry of David A. Reed, one of the authors of this book, ministering primarily to Jehovah's Witnesses. E-mail: davereed@webshowplace.com   Web page: http://www.webshowplace.com.comments

MacGregor Ministries, P.O. Box 73, Balfour, B.C. VOG 1C0, Canada

Mormonism Research Ministry, P.O. Box 20705, El Cajon, CA 92021

Personal Freedom Outreach, P.O. Box 26062, St. Louis, MO 63136

Utah Lighthouse Ministries, P.O. Box 1884, Salt Lake City, UT 84110

Utah Missions, P.O. Box 348, Marlow, OK 73055

Watchman Fellowship, P.O. Box 13251, Arlington, TX 76094

Note: Those listed above represent only a sampling of the many local ministries and support groups—primarily the largest, those staffed by former Mormons, and those most likely to be able to refer inquirers to sources of help closer to home. For a more complete list of such ministries and support groups, please see the *Directory of Cult Research Organizations,* published by American Religions Center, P.O. Box 168, Trenton, MI 48183.

The authors of this book have listings of hundreds of contacts across the United States. If you wish to find help in your locality, or if you have questions or comments concerning this book, you may write John R. Farkas, Berean Christian Ministries, P.O. Box 1091, Webster, NY 14580. E-mail address: bcmmin@frontiernet.net Our web page: http://www.frontiernet.net/~bcmmin

Notes

Preface

1. Calculated by the authors from data in *1993–1994 Church Almanac*, Deseret News, 1992, pp. 395, 399, 400; and *1985 Church Almanac*, Deseret News, 1984, p. 252.

2. *Church News* (April 13, 1996), 6.

3. *Instructions for the Discussions, Uniform System for Teaching the Gospel* (Salt Lake City: The Church of Jesus Christ of Latter-day Saints, 1986), 8, 9, 14, 16, 18, and discussions 1 through 6.

Chapter 1: Witnessing to Mormons

1. You may obtain free copies of up to four pages (on two sheets) from Berean Christian Ministries, P.O. Box 1091, Webster, NY 14580. With your request include a long, self-addressed envelope with two ounces ($0.55) of stamps affixed. Be specific about the title, volume, and page numbers that you need.

2. Some may be concerned about this, citing 2 John 1:10 ("receive him not into your house, neither bid him God speed") as reasons not to admit Mormons. Taken to its extreme, this idea would mean you should not invite anyone into your home who is not a Bible-believing Christian. This would have to include your atheist neighbor, the agnostic pipefitter that you called in to repair your plumbing, and your non-Christian uncle.

Keep in mind that there were no church facilities in biblical times as we know them now (see Philem. 2; Rom. 16:5; Acts 10:5–6; Luke 9:4–5). In those days a houseguest might stay for a few days rather than a few hours, and hospitality often included supplying and equipping the traveling preacher for the next leg of his journey. Second John 1:10 was a warning to people not to let their homes be used as a missionary center or church if those coming to them brought a different doctrine or a different gospel.

Chapter 2: Introduction to Mormonism

1. Bruce R. McConkie, *Mormon Doctrine* (Salt Lake City: Deseret Book Co., 1979).

184

2. "In order of their precedence, beginning at the top, the general authorities of the Church include members of: The First Presidency, Council of the Twelve, the Patriarch to the Church, Assistants to the Twelve, First Council of the Seventy and Presiding Bishopric" (ibid., 309).

3. A key opens something that was closed (Judg. 3:25; Isa. 22:22; Luke 11:52; Rev. 3:7, 9:1, 20:1). The Bible also uses keys as signs of authority (Matt. 16:19; Rev. 1:18). The Book of Mormon does not use the term *keys* as authority and only uses the word once (1 Nephi 4:20), as a literal key.

4. "What Every Elder Should Know—and Every Sister as Well," *Ensign* (February 1993), 7.

5. These statements are found in appendix 4.

6. Even the LDS scripture Doctrine and Covenants tells us to use our intellect: "Whatever principle of intelligence we attain unto in this life, it will rise with us in the resurrection" (D&C 130:18); "The glory of God is intelligence, or, in other words, light and truth" (D&C 93:36); "But, behold, I say unto you, that you must study it out in your mind; then you must ask me if it be right, and if it is right I will cause that your bosom shall burn within you; therefore, you shall feel that it is right" (D&C 9:8). You will not usually hear these used relative to the Book of Mormon.

Chapter 3: For Potential Converts and New Mormons

1. Although the Bible does speak about apostasy in several places (e.g., Matt. 24:11; Acts 20:29–30) nowhere does it say it would be "complete," as taught by the Mormon Church.

2. See *The Church As Organized by Jesus Christ*, 1982; *The Falling Away and Restoration of the Gospel of Jesus Christ Foretold*, 1972; *Which Church Is Right?* 1982 (pp. 9–18). All three booklets (tracts) were published by the Church of Jesus Christ of Latter-day Saints.

3. A good question to ask is, "If the Mormon Church has had a prophet in touch with God since 1830, why do they not have a corrected edition of the Bible that has been made a part of their standard works to replace the King James Version now used?" For more on the reliability of the Bible, see Josh McDowell, *Evidence That Demands a Verdict* and *More Evidence That Demands a Verdict*, (San Bernardino, CA: Campus Crusade for Christ, 1972, 1975).

4. For a brief discussion and some examples, see our book, *Mormonism: Changes, Contradictions and Errors* (Grand Rapids: Baker, 1995), 119–129. For a detailed review of the changes, see Jerald and Sandra Tanner, *3,913 Changes in the Book of Mormon* (Salt Lake City: Utah Lighthouse Ministry, n.d.).

5. For a brief discussion and some examples, see our books *Mormonism: Changes, Contradictions and Errors* (pp. 131–147) and *How to Rescue Your Loved One from Mormonism* (Grand Rapids: Baker, 1994), 101–136. For more details see Jerald and Sandra Tanner, *Mormonism—Shadow or Reality?* (Salt Lake City: Utah Lighthouse Ministry, 1987), 15–31.

6. On December 22, 1994, I (John) requested such information (a booklet or similar) from the Mormon Church headquarters in Salt Lake City. On February 8, 1995, I received two booklets, *The Prophet Joseph Smith's Testimony* and *The Church of Jesus Christ of Latter-day Saints—An Apostle's Testimony,* and two books, Book of Mormon and *Gospel Principles.* On March 25, 1995, we received two more booklets, *The Purpose of Life* and *The Prophet Joseph Smith's Testimony,* and a small book, *Truth Restored.* The booklets contained just a few of the very unique LDS teachings. On April 17, 1996, while on a visit to the Hill Cumorah visitors center, I made a similar request for a small booklet, or similar, that summarized LDS teachings. They had nothing different than was sent from Salt Lake City.

7. Note in Alma 31:15-38 that those who say God is a spirit are not corrected in the prayer of the prophet involved, even though other errors are. In none of the references are any of the speakers corrected for calling God a "spirit" or the "Great Spirit." In Alma 18:26-29, 22:8-11 alleged prophets of God call God the "Great Spirit." The following verses also support the teaching that God is a spirit: ". . . the Father and Son-And they are one God, yea, the very Eternal Father of heaven and earth. And thus the flesh becoming subject to the Spirit, or the Son to the Father, being one God. . . ." (Mosiah 15:3-5).

In the 1835 Doctrine and Covenants, Joseph Smith said the Father was a personage of spirit, as contrasted with the Son, who is a personage of tabernacle (a physical body):

> . . . We shall, in this lecture speak of the Godhead: we mean the Father, Son and Holy Spirit. There are two personages. . . . They are the Father and the Son: The Father being a personage of spirit, glory and power: possessing all perfection and fulness: The Son, who was in the bosom of the Father, a personage of tabernacle . . . And he being the only begotten of the Father . . . possessing the same mind with the Father, which mind is the Holy Spirit. . . . (Lecture Fifth of Faith, 5:1-2, pp. 52-53, 1st edition.)

Not only do the above say that God the Father is a spirit, but there are no LDS scriptures from 1830 to roughly 1842 that contradict them.

8. Copyright 1986 by Corporation of the President of the Church of Jesus Christ of Latter-day Saints. Each has a different title, but the subtitle of each is "Uniform System for Teaching the Gospel."

9. *Church Almanac, Deseret News,* 1989-1990 edition, p. 202; 1993-1994 edition, pp. 306, 390-395, 401; *Church News* (January 6): 1996, 5.

10. The Pearl of Great Price did not exist in 1837.

11. Baptism for the dead is one of the major unique teachings of the Mormon Church that is taught incompletely to prospective new members (missionary discussions vol. 4, page 10 and vol. 6, pages 1, 8, 14). It is a complex idea that to be properly evaluated calls for an understanding of several important principles in the Mormon gospel. These include the importance of baptism, our pre-existence in a pre-mortal state, a full understanding of eternal progression, obedience to God, and priesthood authority. Baptism for the dead

is not the "milk" of the Mormon gospel, yet it is taught, however briefly, prior to baptism.

12. "Thou Shalt Not Bear False Witness," *Ensign* (October 1994): 54.

13. Additional information on this subject can be found in *How to Rescue Your Loved One from Mormonism* (pp. 63–74) and Jerald and Sandra Tanner, *Mormonism—Shadow or Reality*, pp. 97–125.

14. *The Latter-Day Saints' Millennial Star*, "History of Joseph Smith," 16:296.

15. *Teachings of the Prophet Joseph Smith*, p. 345; *Journal of Discourses*, 4:215, 6:3; *History of the Church*, 6:305.

16. Apostle Joseph Fielding Smith (Salt Lake City: Deseret Book Co., 1967), 345–46. This quote is also found in *History of the Church*, 6:305; *Journal of Discourses*, 6:3.

17. *Search These Commandments*, Melchizedek Priesthood Personal Study Guide (Salt Lake City: Church of Jesus Christ of Latter-day Saints, 1984), 152. The question to ask is: "Who is the God of this woman and of the father of God the Father?" It appears that, according to Mormonism, the Son, Jesus Christ, not only has a father, but he also has grandparents, great grandparents, etc.

18. *Achieving a Celestial Marriage* (Corporation of the President of the Church of Jesus Christ of Latter-day Saints, 1976, 1992), 132.

19. A Mormon at this point might say: "The person making this statement is an apostate Zoramite; he is not stating correct doctrine." Yes, it is a Zoramite speaking in this verse, and the missionary Alma does have to correct many of their teachings, but the part about God's being a spirit is not corrected. In fact, the chapter heading does not mention this part of the Zoramite teachings as being in error.

20. Later, on page 55 of this same quote, the idea of there being only two personages is restated again. On pages 53 and 54 we learn that the Holy Ghost is the mind shared by the Father and Son. That there are only two personages is also supported by 2 Nephi 32:3–5; Alma 34:38; 39:6; and D&C 88:3, where the Holy Ghost is called an *it*. An *it* is obviously not a personage. All of these references are from 1835 or earlier. The Holy Ghost being a personage was a later addition to Mormon teachings. Doctrine and Covenants 130:22, which calls the Holy Ghost a personage, is dated April 1843; however, it was not published in any of the LDS periodicals of the period and probably not generally distributed to the general LDS members until after 1855 (Journal of Discourses 3:39, 18:291–292; 23:173). It did not find its way into LDS scripture until the 1876 edition of the D&C and was not accepted by the membership until the October 1880 General Conference (*The Ensign* [December 1984]: 37–38).

21. The Lectures on Faith were in the D&C from 1835 to 1920, when they were quietly removed from the 1921 and following editions.

22. Perhaps a better way to say this is "God is spirit" (John 4:24 New Revised Standard Version).

23. The following biblical verses say the same thing:

The eternal God is thy refuge, and underneath are the everlasting arms: and he shall thrust out the enemy from before thee; and shall say, Destroy them. (Deut. 33:27)

Before the mountains were brought forth, or ever thou hadst formed the earth and the world, even from everlasting to everlasting, thou art God. (Ps. 90:2)

Thy throne is established of old: thou art from everlasting. (Ps. 93:2)

But the mercy of the LORD is from everlasting to everlasting. (Ps. 103:17)

Also see Hosea 11:9, Numbers 23:19, and 1 Samuel 15:29; these all say that God is not man.

24. Old Testament references that have small capitals in the word *Lord* should create complications from a Mormon's point of view. The Lord, according to LDS teachings, is the pre-incarnate Jesus Christ (*Mormon Doctrine*, p. 392; see also "Jehovah" in "Bible Dictionary" in the back of the LDS edition of *The Holy Bible*, 1979). This Isaiah reference and the one just below it (44:6, 8) have the pre-incarnate Jesus Christ saying he does not know anything about his father and his grandfather, his great-great grandfather, and so on, who are also Gods, according to LDS teachings (*Search These Commandments*, Melchizedek Priesthood Personal Study Guide, p. 152; *Achieving a Celestial Marriage*, pp. 129–132; *The Seer*, p. 132).

25. This should also create a problem for temple Mormons, those LDS members who have been to a Mormon temple for their endowments. In this very sacred ceremony, in the creation scene, the pre-incarnate Jesus Christ is shown taking direction from Elohim (the Father) and is assisted in the creation by Michael, who is Adam of the garden of Eden (see *Mormon Doctrine*, p. 17).

26. On pages 4 and 5 of the LDS teaching manual *Gospel Principles* (pre–1986 editions) is a picture of what appears to be a spiral galaxy. It has a caption and text that says: "Our Heavenly Father rules the universe" and ". . . God is the almighty ruler of the universe." If God the Father now has a father, then what would his father (or the God of his father) be in charge of? Many Mormons would say he is in charge of another universe. However the word *universe* by its root means "all together, all taken collectively, the whole." *Webster's Deluxe Unabridged Dictionary*, second edition, also has as its first definition: "the totality of all things that exist; the cosmos; creation."

27. For more on D&C 130:22 see the beginning of chapter 4, under "Joseph Smith's King Follett Address." D&C 121:28 (dated March 20, 1839) says, "A time to come in the which nothing shall be withheld, whether there be one God

or many gods, they shall be manifest." Perhaps this indicates some doubt on Joseph Smith's part about the nature of God.

28. "And this is life eternal, that they might know thee the only true God, and Jesus Christ" (John 17:3). There is a penalty for those who do not know God: "In flaming fire taking vengeance on them that know not God, and that obey not the gospel of our Lord Jesus Christ" (2 Thess. 1:8).

29. Which is the real "first principle"? The fourth item in *The Articles of Faith*, in the Pearl of Great Price (a Mormon scripture), says: "We believe that the first principles and ordinances of the Gospel are: first, Faith in the Lord Jesus Christ; second, Repentance; third, Baptism by immersion for the remission of sins; fourth, Laying on of hands for the gift of the Holy Ghost" (p. 60).

30. Bruce R. McConkie, *Mormon Doctrine* (Bookcraft, 1991 [1966]), 546.

31. Ibid., 742.

32. Box Elder Stake Conference, December 20, 1914. As quoted in *Brigham City Box Elder News* (Jan. 28, 1915): 1–2, as quote in *Family Home Evening*, 1972 pp. 125–126.

33. For the Sunday schools of the Church of Jesus Christ of Latter-Day Saints, Gospel Doctrine Class (Deseret Sunday School Union, Deseret News Press, 1967), 378–79.

The Book of Mormon in Alma 7:10 says that Jesus was conceived by the power of the Holy Ghost, but this is expanded on by the above teachings. Apostle Bruce R. McConkie, in *Mormon Doctrine*, also said, "Our Lord was the only mortal person ever born to a virgin" (p. 822). But here again, the word *virgin* must mean something different in light of the above quotes. It seems that in Mormonism a woman is a virgin even after a physical sexual act with an immortal God, but not with a mortal man.

34. *Journal of Discourses* 2:210.

35. *Journal of Discourses* 4:259.

36. *Journal of Discourses* 1:346.

37. *The Seer,* 1:10:159.

38. These brackets are in the quote.

39. Page 291 in 1986 edition or older; page 303 in the 1992 edition.

Chapter 4: For Non-Mormons and Mormons

1. We say *seems* because from our experience, many LDS members apparently find it hard to admit they do not know all or most of the history and unique teachings. In actuality they have a *testimony* of the Mormon Church because of *feelings* they have, rather than a faith based on factual knowledge.

2. *Teachings of the Prophet Joseph Smith,* p. 345; *History of the Church,* 6:305; *Journal of Discourses,* 6:3.

3. *Fourth Lecture of Faith,* p. 51, and Part Second, Covenants and Commandments Section 2:2, 4–5 (these are now D&C 20:12, 17, 28); 1 Nephi 10:18; 2 Nephi 29:9; Mosiah 3:5, 8; Moroni 7:22, 8:18; Mormon 9:9, 19.

4. *The Ensign* (December 1984): 37–38.

5. *Fifth Lecture of Faith*, p. 52; Part Second, Covenants and Command-ments Section 82:4 (82:4 is now D&C 93:23); and in the Book of Mormon, Alma 18:26–29, 19; 25–27; Mosiah 15:5 in the present edition.

6. *Ensign* (December 1984): 38–39; Richard S. Van Wagoner, *Mormon Polygamy—A History* (Salt Lake City: Signature Books, 1986), 6f., 183f.; "LDS Church Authority and New Plural Marriages 1890–1904," by D. Michael Quinn, *Dialogue* 18, no. 1 (Spring 1985): 9–105.

7. *Achieving a Celestial Marriage*, pp. 129–132; *Gospel Principles*, p. 9; *Articles of Faith*, p. 443.

8. See D&C 130:22; *Teachings of The Prophet Joseph Smith*, p. 370. In fact, the Book of Mormon teaches there is only one God, not three: In the front pages, see the last sentence of "The Testimony of the Three Witnesses"; Alma 11:28–29, 44; 3 Nephi 11:27, 36; Mormon 7:7.

9. Actually they are polytheists, because they teach that there are many gods and that men may become gods.

10. This idea of the three Mormon Gods (Father, Son, Holy Ghost) being one in purpose is found in *Times and Seasons*, 6:1095; McConkie, *Mormon Doctrine*, p. 317; Bruce R. McConkie, *The Promised Messiah*, pp. 5–6.

11. *Teachings of the Prophet Joseph Smith*, p. 345; *Journal of Discourses*, 6:3; *History of the Church*, 6:305.

12. See the *Bible Dictionary*, in *The Holy Bible* published by the Church of Jesus Christ of Latter-day Saints, p. 681 under "God," and p. 711 under "Jehovah."

13. Apostle James E. Talmage, *The Articles of Faith*, pp. 465–473; Boyd Kirkland, "Elohim and Jehovah in Mormonism and the Bible," *Dialogue*, A Journal of Mormon Thought 19, [no. 1 (Spring 1986): 77–93]; Boyd Kirk-land, "Jehovah As The Father," *Sunstone*, 19 [no. 2, Autumn 1984): 36–44].

14. *Deseret News* (Sept. 21, 1856): 235; very similar to *Journal of Dis-courses*, 4:53–54.

15. *Journal of Discourses*, 3:247.

16. *Journal of Discourses*, 4:220.

17. See Jerald and Sandra Tanner, *Mormonism—Shadow or Reality*, 5th ed. (Salt Lake City: Utah Lighthouse Ministry, 1984), 403f. On page 403 is described how Ramos Anderson, a Danish man, was blood atoned for adul-tery. Several other examples are also documented.

18. *Church News* (October 9, 1976), p. 11.

19. *Journal of Discourses*, 1:50.

20. *Journal of Discourses*, 26:22–23.

21. *Deseret Weekly News* (June 18, 1873): 308.

22. To research the subject in more depth—perhaps to satisfy a Mormon disturbed by this information and seeking answers—these additional resources are suggested: Culley K. Christensen, M.D., *The Adam-God Maze* (Scottsdale, AZ: Independent Publishers, 1981); Craig L. Tholson, *Adam-God* (Payson, UT: Publishment, 1991); Joseph W. Musser, *Michael Our Father and Our God*

(Salt Lake City: Truth Publishing, 1963); "Unpublished Adam-God Discourses of Brigham Young 1852–1877," *Doctrines of the Priesthood, 2,* no. 1 (Salt Lake City: Colliers Publishing Co., 1991).

23. For more on this subject we recommend John Heinemann and Anson Shupe, *The Mormon Corporate Empire* (Boston: Beacon Press, 1985) and *Mormonism—Shadow or Reality,* pp. 516–527.

24. *Doctrines of Salvation,* 1:188.

25. To our knowledge The Church of Jesus Christ was never used as the name of the Mormon Church.

26. *The Evening and Morning Star* 2, no. 20, p. 160 (May 1834); *History of the Church,* 2:62.

27. Mormons (males and females) who have been through the temple for their endowments are required to wear temple garments almost continually from that time forward. The original temple garment consisted of a one-piece white union suit reaching from the neck to the wrists and ankles. Shortened sleeves (like a t-shirt), legs to the knees, and separate tops and bottoms are now approved. The garments have four symbolic markings: a square on the right breast and a compass on the left, a stitched line over the navel and over the right knee. Masons have said that the breast markings remind them of the square and the compass pressed against the body in those locations during Masonic rituals.

28. The brackets are in the original.

29. For more on 1 Corinthians 15:29, see Reed and Farkas, *Mormons Answered Verse by Verse* (Grand Rapids: Baker, 1992), 85–86.

30. Mormons are very actively involved in genealogy work to identify their kindred dead, and others, in order to perform the proxy temple ceremonies for them. The Prophet Joseph Smith taught: "The greatest responsibility in this world that God has laid upon us is to seek after our dead" (*Teachings of the Prophet Joseph Smith,* p. 356).

31. To reach *exaltation* means to become a God (*Gospel Principles,* p. 290).

32. Also see D&C 138:32–34; 128:5 and *Mormon Doctrine,* pp. 685–687.

Chapter 5: For Mormons

1. In the Pearl of Great Price.

2. On the Vermont–New York border, a little west and south of Rutland, Vermont, near present-day Hampton, New York and Poultney, Vermont. Oliver Cowdery, Joseph Smith's scribe, had lived in Poultney.

3. This community is described as being located between Lake George and the southern extremity of Lake Champlain (*Gazetteer of the State of New York* (J. H. French, 1860), 680. It is estimated that Dresden was about 15 to 20 miles west of Low Hampton.

4. Everett N. Dick, "The Millerite Movement, 1830–1845." In *Adventism In America, a History,* ed. Gary Land (Grand Rapids: Eerdmans, 1986), 8, 34.

5. *1993–1994 Church Almanac, Deseret News,* 1992, p. 396.

6. *Adventism in America*, pp. 13, 25–29.

7. Ibid., 35; *History of the Church* 5:272 footnotes; Frank S. Mead, *Handbook of Denominations—In the United States*, 5th ed. (Nashville: Abingdon, 1980), 20.

8. The Jehovah's Witnesses since the early part of this century have set and reset several dates for Armageddon, the most recent being 1975. More recently a booklet, *88 Reasons Why the Rapture Will Be in 1988*, by Edgar C. Whisenant received wide circulation in the Christian community. Radio evangelist Harold Camping predicted the end for September 1994. In the meantime, less prominent groups and individuals have called attention to other dates. Bill Alnor in his book *Soothsayers of the Second Advent* (Power Books, 1989) provides a detailed review of this subject.

9. *History of the Church*, 5:271–272, 277.

10. For information on the LDS thinking about Joel, see Bruce R. McConkie, *Mormon Doctrine*, p. 716.

11. For more on "the fulness of the Gentiles" see McConkie, *Mormon Doctrine*, pp. 721, 722.

12. The angel's visit and message were allegedly repeated a total of three times.

13. *Joseph Smith—History*, 1:40–41. This allegedly took place in 1823, but it did not appear in this final printed form until 1838.

14. *Joseph Smith—History*, 1:54. This allegedly took place in 1824–1827, but did not appear in its final form until 1838.

15. The same ideas are expressed in D&C 29:9–11, 22–23, Sept. 1830; 64:30, 34, 37, Sept. 1831; 1:4, Nov. 1831; 133:1–2, 17, Nov. 1831; 84:2, 117, Sept. 1832; 86:4, Dec. 1832; 89:2, Feb. 1833; 110:16, April 1836; 112:30, July 1837; 115:4, April 1838 and in *Joseph Smith—Matthew, 1:36–37, 1831.*

16. As covered in D&C 18:27

17. The remaining three apostles were ordained later, Parley P. Pratt on Feb. 21, 1835, and Orson Pratt and Thomas B. Marsh on April 26, 1835 (*History of the Church*, 2:187–191, *Comprehensive History of the Church*, 1:374–375).

18. A sample of 560 LDS blessings in the 1839–1899 period showed that six of the individuals blessed were told they would not taste death and fifty-seven were told they would remain until the Second Coming (Irene M. Bates, "Patriarchal Blessings and the Routinization of Charisma," *Dialogue: A Journal of Mormon Thought* 26, no. 3 [Fall 1993]: 9–11, 20, 21).

19. *Comprehensive History of the Church*, 1:375; *Times and Seasons*, 6:868.

20. Luman Shurtliff Autobiography, 1807–1847, typescript, Brigham Young University—Special Collections Library, p. 44; *LDS Historical Library*, 1992©, by Infobases, Inc.

21. D&C, 1891 ed., in "Covenants and Commandments" 130:15, p. 461, n. 1.

22. Apostle Bruce R. McConkie quotes Joseph Smith in describing the "rising generation" and makes a ridiculous attempt to explain away his obvious prophetic failure:

"I was once praying very earnestly to know the time of the coming of the Son of Man," the Prophet Joseph Smith recorded on April 2, 1843, "when I heard a voice repeat the following: Joseph, my son, if thou livest until thou art eighty-five years old, thou shalt see the face of the Son of Man; therefore let this suffice, and trouble me no more on this matter.

"I was left thus, without being able to decide whether this coming referred to the beginning of the millennium or to some previous appearing, or whether I should die and thus see his face. I believe the coming of the Son of Man will not be any sooner than that time" (D. & C. 130:14–17).

Four days later, April 6, 1843, at the General Conference of the Church, while the Spirit rested upon him, the Prophet said: 'Were I going to prophesy, I would say the end would not come in 1844, 5, or 6, or in forty years. **There are those of the rising generation who shall not taste death till Christ comes."**

The rising generation is the one that has just begun. Thus, technically, children born on April 6, 1843, would be the first members of the rising generation, and all children born, however many years later, to the same parents would still be members of that same rising generation. It is not unreasonable to suppose that many young men had babies at the time of this prophecy and also had other children as much as 50 or 75 years later, assuming for instance that they were married again to younger women. This very probable assumption would bring the date up to, say, the 2nd decade in the 20th century—and the children so born would be members of that same rising generation of which the Prophet spoke. Now if these children lived to the normal age of men generally they would be alive well past the year 2000 A.D. (*Mormon Doctrine*, pp. 692–693).

23. *History of the Church*, 5:336–337, April 6, 1843; *Teachings of the Prophet Joseph Smith*, p. 286. Joseph Smith was born December 23, 1805, which means the Lord would come after December 23, 1890.

24. Martha Thomas was born in 1808; hence she would be 80 years old in 1888. This is close to the 1890 time frame that results from other sources. Note that this statement is similar to the promise given to the three apostles in their 1835 blessing (Martha Thomas autobiography, in *Daniel Thomas Family History*, 1927, pp. 32–33; *LDS Historical Library*, 1992©, by Infobases, Inc.).

25. The brackets are in the quote.

26. *The Discourses of Wilford Woodruff*, 1946, 1990, pp. 252–256.

27. It seems that when the Lord did not come in the 1891 period, LDS leaders continued a positive outlook. A small sampling of examples of these are found in *Gospel Standards*, Heber J. Grant, 1941, pp. 18, 81; Harold B. Lee, *Conference Report*, April 1966, p. 64; N. Eldon Tanner, *Conference Report*, October 1968, p. 46; Joseph Fielding Smith, *Conference Report*, April 1969, p. 121; *Teachings of Ezra Taft Benson*, 1988, pp. 19–20.

28. These brackets are in the quote. *The Teachings of Ezra Taft Benson*, 1988, p. 20.

29. The Book of Mormon claims that after his ascension to heaven in Israel, our Lord Jesus Christ made a bodily visit to the New World:

And it came to pass that in the ending of the thirty and fourth year, behold, I will show unto you that the people of Nephi who were spared, and also those who had been called Lamanites, who had been spared, did have great favors shown unto them, and great blessings poured out upon their heads, insomuch **that soon after the ascension of Christ into heaven he did truly manifest himself unto them— Showing his body unto them, and ministering unto them; and an account of his ministry shall be given hereafter. Therefore for this time I make an end of my sayings.** (3 Nephi 10:18–19)

And it came to pass that when Jesus had spoken these words the whole multitude fell to the earth; for they remembered that it had been prophesied among them that Christ should show himself unto them after his ascension into heaven. And it came to pass that the Lord spake unto them saying: Arise and come forth unto me, that ye may thrust your hands into my side, and also that ye may feel the prints of the nails in my hands and in my feet, that ye may know that I am the God of Israel, and the God of the whole earth, and have been slain for the sins of the world. (3 Nephi 11:12–14)

There are problems with this idea. The Mormon and Christian communities have been expecting the Lord's second coming. Based on the Book of Mormon the Mormons should be looking for the Lord's third coming, not the second coming. Secondly, Jesus sent his apostles and disciples to "all the world" and "among all nations" (Matt. 28:19; Mark 16: 15; Luke 24:47–48). What kind of leader would give his people a responsibility and then take it away without telling them? And to be fair and consistent, would he not also have to visit all the other major continents, like Asia, Europe, Australia and Japan?

30. *Joseph Smith History* 1:10. It is interesting to note that just eight verses later Joseph Smith said: "for at this time it had never entered into my heart that all were wrong" (*Joseph Smith—History,* 1:18).

31. *Ensign* (Dec. 1984): 38; *Encyclopedia of Mormonism* 3:1071, under Pearl of Great Price.

32. Joseph Smith-History 1:1–20 (pp. 47–50, 1981 ed.).

33. *Ensign* (Dec. 1984): 24–26 (Jan. 1985): 11; *The Personal Writings of Joseph Smith,* ed. Dean C. Jessee (Salt Lake City, Deseret Book Co.), 4–6.

34. *Times and Seasons* Vol. 3, No. 10 (March 15, 1842): 726–728 and Vol. 3, No. 11 (April 1, 1842): 748–749.

35. First published by the Utah Christian Tract Society, it is currently available from Mormonism Research Ministry, P.O. Box 20705, El Cajon, CA 92021.

36. Salt Lake City: Smith Research Associates, 1994 (distributed by Signature Books), pp. 15–41.

37. Oliver Cowdery was Joseph Smith's scribe for most of the writing of the Book of Mormon, was present during the alleged restoration of the priesthood, and was the "second elder," i.e., the number two man in the whole church.

38. This paper's paging started with 1 at the start of the October 1834 edition and continued increasing with each paper's publication. The new edition continued the page numbering where the previous one left off.

39. Preliminary draft of "Lucy Smith's History," page 55 of the handwritten copy, page 174 of the typed transcript in the LDS Archives, Salt Lake City. This was published in a greatly modified form under *"History of Joseph Smith"* by his mother Lucy Mack Smith, Bookcraft, 1958.

40. "Lucy Smith's History," handwritten copy, pp. 46–47.

41. *Quarterly Journal,* Personal Freedom Outreach, Vol. 8, No. 1 (Jan.–March, 1987): 4.

42. All men were required to spend a given time each year on road maintenance. Joseph Smith Sr. first appeared on the Palmyra records in April 1817 and then again for the same location in 1818 and 1819. But in 1820 the senior Smith's name appears at the end of the list, showing that he had moved and was still living in Palmyra, but 50 feet north of the Palmyra-Farmington town line. In April 1820, Alvin Smith's name (Joseph's brother) first appears. Hyrum first appears 1821 when they reached the age of 21. Alvin and the senior Smith are still on the records in April 1822. Tax records show that they purchased the property for their farm in late 1820 or early 1821 (*Inventing Mormonism,* pp. 1–8).

43. Cited by Marquardt and Walters, *Inventing Mormonism,* pp. xxv and 7.

44. J. H. French, LL.D., *Gazetteer of the State of New York,* 1860, p. 497; Horatio Gates Spafford, *Gazetteer of the State of New York,* LL.D., 1824, p. 302.

45. These were not college teachers, but church members. See more on this in chapter 6 in "Answering Questions and Objections from Mormons."

46. The brackets are in the quote. The Book of Mormon publication process started in 1827; see appendix 2 for the dates associated with the Book of Mormon.

47. These two articles were reported in Francis W. Kirkham, *A New Witness for Christ in America* (Independence, MO: Zion Printing and Publishing Co., 1942), 281–295; and Fawn M. Brodie, *No Man Knows My History* (New York: Alfred A. Knopf, 1974), 22–23, 429–31.

48. Donna Hill, *Joseph Smith, The First Mormon* (New York: Doubleday 1977), 48; D. Michael Quinn, *Early Mormonism and the Magic World View* (Salt Lake City: Signature Books, 1987), 38–50, 122–123, 143–148, 194–214.

49. "And again, thou shalt take thy brother, Hiram Page, between him and thee alone, and tell him that those things which he hath written from that stone are not of me and that Satan deceiveth him;" (Sept. 1830, Doctrine and Covenants 28:11 also note the historical heading in the orginal, not shown, of this revelation; *History of the Church,* 1:111)

EARLY SPECULATION AS TO SITE OF NEW JERUSALEM. When it was made known that the New Jerusalem was to be built in America, the saints began to wonder where the city would be. Hiram Page, one of the witnesses of the Book of Mormon, secured a "peep stone" by means of which he claimed to receive revelation for the Church. Among the things he attempted to make known was where this city was to be built. Considerable commotion naturally prevailed, and even Oliver Cowdery was deceived into accepting what Hiram Page had given. The Prophet Joseph Smith had some difficulty in correcting this evil and composing the minds of the members of the Church. (*Doctrines of Salvation*, Joseph Fielding Smith Jr., 3:75)

Hiram Page—Born in Vermont 1800; baptized April 11, 1830; withdrew from the Church, 1838; died in Ray Co., Missouri, August 12, 1852. (*The Articles of Faith*, James E. Talmage, p. 503)

To our great grief, however, we soon found that Satan had been lying in wait to deceive, and seeking whom he might devour. Brother Hiram Page had in his possession a certain stone, by which he had obtained certain revelations concerning the upbuilding (sic) of Zion, the order of the Church, etc., . . . (*History of the Church*, 1:109–110)

50. Hill, *Joseph Smith, The First Mormon*, p. 48.

51. "Smith's accounts of this first vision were consistent with other contemporary ecstatic experiences; nothing about his account was unusual for his time and place." D. Michael Quinn, *The Mormon Hierarchy* (Salt Lake City: Signature Books, 1994), 3. In note 13 on page 269 of this same reference, several examples are given.

52. Karl Ricks Anderson, *Joseph Smith's Kirtland* (Salt Lake City: Deseret Books, 1989), 107–113.

53. Marvin Hill, "The First Vision Controversy: A Critique and Reconciliation," *Dialogue, A Journal of Mormon Thought* 15, no. 2 (Summer 1982): 39. This article is also available from Mormon Miscellaneous, 8865 South 1300 East, Sandy, UT 84092, March 1986, Reprint 7, p. 9.

54. Credit for the general approach in this section belongs to author Mark J. Cares who discussed it in his book *Speaking the Truth in Love to Mormons* (Milwaukee: Northwestern Publishing House, 1993), 170–184.

55. *Gospel Principles*, p. 290; *Achieving a Celestial Marriage*, pp. 129–132.

56. *The New Testament Study Bible—Matthew* (The Complete Biblical Library, Springfield, MO: 1989), 101–102.

57. See the end of appendix 5 for more on the JST.

58. The same idea is in the JST of this verse. Another example is: "Brethren, I beseech you to **be perfect as I am perfect; for I am persuaded as ye have a knowledge of me, ye have not injured me at all by your sayings.**" JST Gal. 4:12.

59. The same idea is in the JST of this verse.

60. From John 20:26–28 we learn that after his resurrection Jesus Christ continued to show the marks of the nails in his hands and the cut in his side. Does this mean he was not "perfect"?

61. The *Encyclopedia of Mormonism*, 3:1316, in describing "Sin" says: "To overcome sin and be forgiven are to **forsake ungodliness, to acknowledge dependence on God, and to seek to do his will.**"

62. The word *save* to a Mormon in most cases means just being resurrected, but it can also mean reaching exaltation, becoming a God in the top level of the celestial kingdom, the place where the Mormon God the Father dwells. For this reason, it is important not to use jargon. Explain to the Mormon the sense in which you are using the term *saved*.

63. The [JST has the same idea.]

64. "Confess means to acknowledge sin and guilt in the light of God's revelation, and is thus generally an outward sign of repentance and faith." *New Bible Dictionary* (Wheaton, Ill.: Tyndale House, 1962), 225. This same reference, on page 1018, says: "In the NT the words translated 'repent' . . . usually mean 'to change one's mind,' and so also 'to regret, feel remorse.'"

Mormon Apostle Bruce R. McConkie in his book *Mormon Doctrine*, deals with confession under forgiveness:

Forgiveness, which includes divine pardon and complete remission of sins, is available, on conditions of repentance, for all men except those who have sinned unto death. (D. & C. 42:18, 79; 64:7.) For such there is no forgiveness, neither in this world nor in the world to come. (D. & C. 76:32–34; 132:27; Matt. 12:31–32.) To accountable persons in the world, remission of sins comes by repentance and baptism of water and of the Spirit. For those who have once been cleansed in this way and who thereafter commit sin—but not unto death—(and all members of the Church are guilty of sin, in either greater or lesser degree) the law of forgiveness embraces the following requirements:

1. GODLY SORROW FOR SIN. . . . .2. ABANDONMENT OF SIN. . . . .3. CONFESSION OF SIN. . . . .4. RESTITUTION FOR SIN. . . . .5. OBEDIENCE TO ALL LAW.—Complete forgiveness is reserved for those only who **turn their whole hearts to the Lord and begin to keep all of his commandments not just those commandments disobeyed in the past, but those in all fields** . . . (pp. 292–295)

65. Spencer W. Kimball, *The Miracle of Forgiveness* (Salt Lake City: Bookcraft, 1969), 360.

66. "The word 'grace' in its special Christian sense refers to the freedom of salvation in Jesus Christ. As used by Paul in particular, the word underscores the fact that salvation is freely given by God to undeserving sinners." (*The International Standard Bible Encyclopedia* [Grand Rapids: Eerdmans, 1982]) 2:547.

By contrast, *The Encyclopedia of Mormonism*, on the subject of "grace" says: "God bestows these additional, perfecting expressions of grace conditionally, as he does the grace that allows forgiveness of sin. They are given **'after all we can do' (2 Ne. 25:23)—that is, in addition to our best efforts"** (New York: Macmillan, 1992), 2:562.

Biblical grace, on the other hand, is the unmerited forgiveness of God because of our faith in Jesus Christ and our confession and repentance of our sins.

67. The JST has the same idea.

68. "Believeth on the Son"; that is, believe that Jesus is who and what he has revealed himself to be "according to the scriptures," as in 1 Corinthians 15:3–4.

69. The JST has the same idea.

70. Spencer W. Kimball, *The Miracle of Forgiveness*, p. 286.

71. *Achieving a Celestial Marriage*, p. 130.

72. That is, "eternal life," becoming a God, having spirit children, and a planet whose people worship you as we do God the Father (*Gospel Principles*, p. 290, 1986 editions, or older).

73. The word *gospel* has a different meaning to most Mormons. Mormon Apostle Bruce R. McConkie said, "The gospel of Jesus Christ is the plan of salvation. It embraces all of the laws, principles, doctrines, rites, ordinances, acts, powers, authorities, and keys necessary to save and exalt men in the highest heaven hereafter. It is the covenant of salvation which the Lord makes with men on earth." *Mormon Doctrine*, p. 331.

74. The Mormon Church does not recognize the authority of any other church to perform these ordinances.

75. A health law covered in D&C 89.

76. Items 9 and 15 are part of the three major goals of the Mormon Church: perfecting the saints, saving the dead, spreading the gospel (their gospel).

77. *New Bible Dictionary* (Wheaton, IL: Tyndale House, 1962), 1069.

78. For more on Mormon authority see appendixes 1 and 4.

79. 1966 edition, p. 527, under NEGROES; this statement has been taken out of the 1979 edition and has been replaced with the 1978 revelation.

80. August 17, 1949, First Presidency letter, in *Neither White Nor Black*, ed. Lester E. Bush and Armand L Mauss (Salt Lake City: Signature Books), p. 221.

81. D&C 128:14 says the same thing, contradicting D&C 29:32. The JST is similar.

82. Not by a Heavenly Mother!

83. For additional study, see Lester E. Bush Jr., "Mormonism's Negro Doctrine: An Historical Overview," *Dialogue* (Spring 1973): 8:1; Bush and Mauss, eds. *Neither White Nor Black; Mormonism—Shadow or Reality?* pp. 262–293.

Chapter 6: Responses—Mormons' and Yours

1. This quote from a Mormon scripture is part of the "First Vision" story of Joseph Smith that allegedly took place in 1820. It is considered to be the foundation of the Mormon Church, its reason for being. There are more than six different versions of this event.

2. In an official publication of the Mormon Church, Apostle Dallin H. Oaks said, "We affirm that this divine declaration was a condemnation of the creeds, not of the faithful seekers who believed them" ("Apostasy And Restoration," *Ensign* [May 1995]: 85).

3. Mormon Apostle Dallin H. Oaks took this approach in a letter to John Farkas dated June 6, 1995.

4. See *Creeds, Sects and the Mormon Church*, a 10-page booklet by one of the coauthors of this book, John Farkas.

5. *Book of Mormon Student Manual,* Religion 121 and 122 (Prepared by the Church Educational System, published by the Church of Jesus Christ of the Latter-day Saints), p. 14.

6. Elder [Apostle] Mark E. Peterson, *Which Church Is Right?* (Salt Lake City: Church of Jesus Christ of Latter-day Saints, 1982), 17. This tract is no longer in print, but the ideas have not been withdrawn; Mormons still claim to be the one true church. The LDS Church more recently has been actively trying to integrate itself into the Christian community, not because it has changed its teachings but, as we believe, to obtain community respectability and acceptance, thus removing an obstacle to conversions.

7. Salt Lake City: Deseret Book Co., 1985.

8. *Ensign* (May 1978): 77.

9. McConkie, *Mormon Doctrine,* pp. 42–46; *Joseph Smith—History,* 1:18–20; *Encyclopedia of Mormonism* 1:56–58; *The Church as Organized by Jesus Christ,* 1982; *The Falling Away and Restoration of the Gospel of Jesus Christ Foretold,* 1972; *Which Church Is Right,* 1982, pp. 9–18. All three booklets (tracts) were published by the Church of Jesus Christ of Latter-day Saints.

10. *History of the Church* (August 15, 1844), 7:250.

11. See David Reed, *Jehovah's Witnesses Answered Verse by Verse,* Baker Book House, 1986, 1995 printing and Robert Countess, *The Jehovah's Witnesses' New Testament,* Presbytesian and Reformed Publishing Co., Phillipsburg, N.J., second edition, 1987.

12. *Church News* (June 20, 1992): 3.

13. There are many publications that cover a part of the subject. A good starting place is John E. Hallwas and Roger D. Launius, *Cultures in Conflict* (Utah State University Press, Logan, UT 84322-7800, 1995), 1–165.

14. These ideas are expanded on in a private paper, *Creeds, Sects and the Mormon Church,* by John Farkas, July 2, 1992.

15. Salt Lake City: Bookcraft, 1971.

16. The question to ask is: "Who is the God of this woman and of the father of God the Father?" It appears that, according to Mormonism, the Son, Jesus Christ, not only has a father, he also has grandparents, great grandparents etc. *Church News* (Sept. 19, 1936): 2. (*Search These Commandments,* Melchizedek Priesthood Personal Study Guide [Salt Lake City: Church of Jesus Christ of Latter-day Saints, 1984], 152.)

17. D&C 84:16; Abraham 1:3 says Adam is the first man.

Chapter 7: Authors' Testimonies

1. Mormons (males and females) who have been through the temple for their "endowments" are required to wear "temple garments" continually from that time forward. The original temple garment consisted of a one-piece white union suit reaching from the neck to the wrists and ankles. Shortened sleeves (like a t-shirt), knee-length legs, and separate tops and bottoms are now approved. The garments have four symbolic markings: a square on the right

breast and a compass on the left, a stitched line over the navel and over the right knee. Masons have said that the breast markings remind them of the square and the compass pressed against the body in those locations during Masonic rituals.

Appendix 2

1. For more on this, see chapter 5 under "The First Vision."

2. This was by a hearing, but there is no evidence the trial was held.

3. These were removed from the Doctrine and Covenants starting with the 1921 edition.

4. *1993–1994 Church Almanac*, Deseret News, pp. 396–399, 1992.

Appendix 3

1. *Teachings of the Prophet Joseph Smith*, p. 345; *Journal of Discourses*, 4:215, 6:3; *History of the Church*, 6:305.

2. This quote is also found in *History of the Church* 6:305; *Journal of Discourses* 6:3.

Appendix 4

1. The "brethren" at conferences are the General Authorities of the Mormon Church. If what they say is "the mind of the Lord, the will of the Lord, the voice of the Lord, and the power of God unto salvation," then the sayings of the Prophet and President of the Church would be even more so.

2. This verse is used here as the Mormon missionaries use it, not as it is in context.

Appendix 5

1. From the footnote on page 324 and the text on page 341 of the reference, and from D&C 57:1–3, we learn that Zion is in Jackson County, Independence, Missouri, where the new Bible was to be printed.

Subject Index

Scripture Index

Mormon Scripture Index